D1601294

THE TWO SELVES

THE TWO SELVES

Their Metaphysical Commitments and
Functional Independence

Stanley B. Klein

OXFORD
UNIVERSITY PRESS

OXFORD

UNIVERSITY PRESS

Oxford University Press is a department of the University of Oxford.
It furthers the University's objective of excellence in research, scholarship,
and education by publishing worldwide.

Oxford   New York

Auckland   Cape Town   Dar es Salaam   Hong Kong   Karachi
Kuala Lumpur   Madrid   Melbourne   Mexico City   Nairobi
New Delhi   Shanghai   Taipei   Toronto

With offices in

Argentina   Austria   Brazil   Chile   Czech Republic   France   Greece
Guatemala   Hungary   Italy   Japan   Poland   Portugal   Singapore
South Korea   Switzerland   Thailand   Turkey   Ukraine   Vietnam

Oxford is a registered trademark of Oxford University Press
in the UK and certain other countries.

Published in the United States of America by
Oxford University Press
198 Madison Avenue, New York, NY 10016

Library of Congress Cataloging-in-Publication Data
Klein, Stanley B.
The two selves : their metaphysical commitments and functional
independence / Stanley B. Klein.
pages cm
Includes bibliographical references and index.
ISBN 978-0-19-934996-8
1. Self-consciousness (Awareness)   2. Knowledge, Theory of.
3. Metaphysics.   I. Title.
BD450.K587 2013
126—dc23
2013020981

1 3 5 7 9 8 6 4 2
Printed in the United States of America
on acid-free paper

This book is dedicated to my mother, Julia Klein, and my father, Melvin Klein

CONTENTS

PREFACE

Imagine a situation in which there are present three persons: an experimenter, an observer, and you. The experimenter tells you: "Lift your right index finger." You do so. After N seconds, the experimenter again gives the command, and again you obey. This procedure is repeated for a number of trials, over a 15-minute period, with N varying randomly from 2 to 30 seconds. Every time, the observer accurately predicts your behavior: you lift your finger when the command is given, not before it and always after it.

This sort of stimulus-response (S-R) connection is as a nice illustration of an instance of necessary and sufficient conditions for a specific behavioral act—lifting of a finger in a particular situation: Whenever S (the command to lift your finger) occurs, R (lifting your finger) occurs. In the absence of S, R does not occur. We have here a clear and simple demonstration of the validity of the utility of stimulus-response psychology.

Now, let's change the imagined scenario. You still are there, the same observer still is there, but the experimenter is not. The observer sees the same things that he saw before: Over a 15-minute period, you lift your right index finger every now and then, with your responses randomly occurring at intervals between 2 and 30 seconds. However, this time the observer can no longer predict when you are going to lift your finger.

Here is the central question: "In this second scenario, *who* gives the command *to whom* to lift the finger?" One obvious way to capture what is going on is to suggest that the subject now is exercising his or her free will to engage in certain behavior. But this assertion simply describes the situation. It leaves little for further study. More important, to conflate—or just ignore the difference between—two clearly distinguishable aspects of the scenario, issuing a command and executing it, is counterproductive.

A preferable answer to the "who and to whom" question is that the situation can be conceptualized as the interaction between two distinctive components of the brain/mind. One of them "makes up" and issues the finger-lifting command, and the other "listens" and takes action. In this book, the two components of the mind/brain are conceptualized as two kinds of "self." "Self," as the reader probably knows, is the replacement of the earlier pre-scientific concept of the "homunculus." A voluminous literature on the self exists. As employed in contemporary psychology, the term *self* admits to a multitude of descriptions and meanings (e.g., Klein, 2004, 2010, 2012a). There are many ways of studying the self, but there is much confusion—as in the study of *consciousness,* a close family relation of self—although a reasonable degree of progress can be pointed to.

Of course, before speculating on the need to posit two aspects or kinds of selves (the "who" and "to whom") to account for the "finger-lifting scenario," determinist alternatives deserve consideration. Such explanations have the scientific "merit" of avoiding any need to postulate messy aspects of reality such as free will, mind/body differences, or types of selves. A determinist might explain the second version of the scenario (i.e., finger lifting absent the experimenter's commands) by arguing that, while the finger movements were not causally related to the external commands, they were caused by something *other than* an interaction between your two selves. For example, Pierre-Simon Laplace's conception of determinism—according to which an infinitely intelligent demon who knows all the initial conditions and all of the physical laws relevant to your finger movements—suggests that your finger had *no choice* but to move when it did (of course, the phrase "no choice" might seem to reintroduce the question of free will, albeit via a dimly lit back door).

I think Laplace's demon argument—as well as its more recent philosophical variants—ultimately is unsatisfactory. Why? Because one of the premises of most determinist deductions—i.e., if we (a) know all the initial conditions, (b) know all the physically relevant laws, and (c) if we have if an intellect sufficiently sophisticated to subject this information to the correct analyses, then (d) we can predict with certainty the future state of any system—is, by Kurt Gödel's incompleteness theorem (e.g., Nagel & Newman, 2001; Rosser, 1936), false.

According to Gödel's theorem, one cannot supply proofs for all the laws that capture all the truths about *any* formal system from *within* that system. If this is so, then it is impossible to derive the internal consistency of a very large class of deductive systems (although Gödel's theorem was specifically targeted to arithmetic systems, it has been generalized to other internally consistent systems of axioms; for discussion as well as a critique, see Wang, 1996). In other words, for any given set of axioms, there are true mathematical statements that cannot be derived from the set itself: there will always be statements about the system that cannot be proved within the system—hence the name "incompleteness theorem."

Mathematical statements that are assumed true, but cannot be proved within their system of origin, can, according to Gödel's logic, be proved in larger systems that can be shown to be valid forms of reasoning; they are simply undecidable in the more limited system. Thus, one always can seek a meta-formalization to capture all of the "truths" of any closed system. However, this incompleteness can be iterated infinitely. Accordingly, certain laws assumed true within a system of axioms cannot be proven within any finite time due to infinite regression. So, neither you, nor I, nor Laplace's demon can know with mathematical certainty *all* the laws. And if that is the case, then the deductive argument for determinism falls victim to the falsity of premise *b*.[1]

But that is not the only problem. Since precise specification of the fate of any determinist processes depends in a highly sensitive manner on exact knowledge of initial conditions of individual sub-atomic particles, and since, by the principle of quantum indeterminacy (see Chapter 3), knowledge of these conditions can never be obtained with sufficient precision, the equations of motion cannot be solved in an unambiguous manner. (Quantum mechanics makes precise predictions for the probabilities of the outcome of large aggregates of particles, and these probability distributions are deterministic; see, e.g., Thompson, 2008. However, predicting the fate of an individual particle remains indeterminable.) Thus, at the level of individual particles, premise *a* also cannot be realized, except by allowing for margins of error in prediction (which, by virtue of the dynamics of chaos theory, may be considerable).

While the issues raised do not necessarily entail that determinism is false (or that free will is true), neither do they provide much comfort to advocates of a fully deterministic reality. For my purposes, the take-away message is that nothing in the sciences logically precludes the possibility that the "second scenario" of the finger-lifting exercise can be explained by postulating the activities (and causal potencies) of two selves. (Although questions concerning free will and determinism clearly are related to some of the core issues raised in this book, I will not deal with this large, contentious philosophical and psychological literature. We have more than enough to occupy us without opening that particular can of theoretical worms! The interested reader is referred to Balaguer, 2010; Kane, 2002; Libet, 1993; and Swinburne, 2011, for treatments of the role of free will in modern science, psychology, philosophy, and theology.)

The main message of this book is that the self is (a) real, (b) causally potent, and (c) consists of multiple aspects that have different parts to play in experience and behavior. A second, but important, message concerns the need to keep one's mind open to the *possibility* that reality, taken in its fullness, leaves room for aspects that do not admit to material instantiation. With regard to the self, I describe philosophical and psychological evidence in support of the idea that the self of everyday experience consists of two aspects—one material (the neuro-cognitive self) and one immaterial (the self of first-person subjectivity). I hope to show that each is an aspect of reality, that each constitutes a necessary condition for the human experience of "self" and that each has a causal role to play; however, I also argue that these two types of self have very different metaphysical commitments. Whether I succeed in making these points is something you will need to decide after reading what I have to say.

In Chapter 1, I make the case that the self is not, *contra* much psychological and philosophical doctrine, a "thing" to be studied. Rather, it is a multiplicity of aspects consisting of both neural-cognitive (largely, but not exclusively, memory-based) instantiations as well as first-person subjectivity. I argue that the former aspect of self is material in nature and objectifiable, and thus amenable to scientific scrutiny. In contrast, the latter aspect of self is an immaterial subjectivity and thus not (easily) captured by the materialist dogma of modern science.

Chapter 2 describes more fully the neuro-cognitive aspect of self and presents evidence for the functional independence of its component systems (e.g., semantic self-facts, semantic trait self-knowledge, and episodic self-narratives). Much of this empiricism comes from my laboratory. For this, I apologize. I am one of the leading researchers on such matters (akin to being "king of the ant hill"—a rather small kingdom!), so the reader will have to suffer through an excess of "Klein" studies.

In Chapter 3, I describe the self of first-person experience and explore the *possibility* that this aspect of self might exist in non-material form. The position of modern science is that all of reality is ultimately material. However, as Meixner (2005) demonstrates in a carefully crafted analysis, materialism is a metaphysical position, not a scientific fact. The materialist stance is an example of what Rescher (1984) classifies as a scientific precommitment — that is, a *presumption* that helps determine the formative background of the questions we ask nature, rather than a *fact* we discover by virtue of the answers we receive (see also Hanson, 1958). Accordingly, a materialist stance does not have a greater claim on our credence than any other metaphysical position.

Many of the arguments I present in support of the *possibility* of immaterial aspects of reality draw on the principles of quantum indeterminancy and relativity theory. It is somewhat ironic, but curiously satisfying, that science itself provides some of the theoretical machinery and logical concepts needed to make discussion of the possibility of a reality that supersedes the limitations of science feasible (as the reader may have noticed, this outcome has a decidedly Gödelian flavor!).

My arguments for the immateriality of the subjective aspect of self do not amount to a proof. Rather, they should be taken only as an appeal to broaden our appreciation of what might constitute reality. While I hope to convince you that here are things that the materialist stance of modern science cannot explain (e.g., Gendlin, 1962; Martin, 2008; Papa-Grimaldi, 1998), recognition of limitations is not the same as offering an alternative. But the recognition of those limits is a precondition to at least being open to alternatives (Nagel, 2012). One alternative, discussed in this book, is the possibility that there exists a conscious, immaterial aspect of reality—i.e., that consciousness, as exemplified by what I call the "ontological self" (see Chapter 1), is a central feature of nature rather than an epiphenomenon to be explained away via a materialist reductive analysis. Whether my arguments are sufficient to support this alternative approach to "what is real" is something you will have to judge for yourself. The best I can realistically hope for is that my arguments will convince you to leave open the metaphysical door, not that they will enable you to identify with certainty what passes through it.

In Chapter 4, I provide a brief—but, I believe, much needed—summary of the two aspects of self: the epistemological (i.e., the material) and ontological (i.e., the immaterial). My justification—if one allows me considerable leeway in the meaning and use of that word—for this unusual nomenclature for the two aspects of the self is provided in Chapter 1.

Chapter 5 considers arguments for the need for both psychological and material aspects of reality. I then present evidence from case studies (e.g., patients suffering anosognosia,

PREFACE

depersonalization, schizophrenic thought-insertion) showing that one can lose one's sense of personal ownership of one's mental states (e.g., "the thought/memory is in my head, but it is not mine!") while still maintaining a clear *sense* of one's material and immaterial self. This dissociation, I argue, hints that the "feeling of personal ownership" may be what unites these two metaphysically separable aspects of self.

In Chapter 6, I summarize the points made in previous chapters. I also appeal for a more inclusive approach to the empirical study of psychological reality—an approach that considers *all* aspects of experience as real, and attempts to understand those experiences using *all* the tools currently available. Finally, I conclude that the self of neural instantiation and the self of subjectivity are contingently related by personal ownership, and that this connection can be undone under certain conditions of pathology. This suggests, in turn, a functional independence of, and reality for, the two categories of self discussed in this book.

The possibility of an immaterial aspect of reality will, in all likelihood, be seen by readers as the most polarizing part of this book. The idea that an immaterial, conscious self might have a categorical irreducibility that is impossible to explain in terms of other categories of nature—such as mass, time, and space—has gained traction in recent years. Chalmers (1996), for instance, opined that a new ontology, in which consciousness is accorded the status of a fundamental aspect of reality, might be needed. But not everyone is comfortable granting the *immaterial* entry into a reality that is taken by modern science to be exclusively *material*. Materialist-minded folk (the majority of scientists and Western philosophers) will thus look away; those steeped in Eastern contemplative traditions will wonder what the fuss is about; and theologians will find in the immaterial self a potential opening for discussion about the reality of the soul.

I agree with my theological friends that the possibility of an immaterial, consciousness self does have certain affinities with the concept of a "soul." However, I do not think the concept of immateriality explored in this book should be affiliated with any *particular* religious tradition, doctrine, or denomination. Immaterial self-consciousness, if it exists, may very well be capable of being related to a particular set of theological principles, but such a maneuver requires a rather Procrustean manipulation of the ideas presented herein.

ACKNOWLEDGMENTS

Many people have contributed both directly and indirectly to the ideas in this book. My deep gratitude goes to Moshe Lax, whose belief in my work combined with his financial support helped bring this book to fruition. Of great importance is Endel Tulving (who provided the "finger lifting" scenario that opens the Preface). I feel very fortunate to be able to consider Endel, in chronological order, a mentor, colleague, and friend. In terms of personal importance, the ordering would be reversed. Without Endel's support, encouragement, and feedback, I doubt seriously this project would have been undertaken.

I have benefited enormously from the insightful suggestions and gentle corrections from a truly gifted group of philosophers and psychologists. They generously gave of their time on what may have seemed to them a rather curious (and perhaps ill-conceived) project. Thanks are due to Robin Collins, David Funder, Byron Kaldis, Tim Lane, Marya Schechtman, Galen Strawson, and Richard Swinburne. I also want to express my gratitude to Carl Craver, Jonardon Ganeri, Shaun Nichols, and Dan Zahavi.

Although they were not directly involved in the writing of this book, our conversations have been invaluable for my understanding of the general issues involved.

I thank Joan Bossert and Miles Osgood, my wonderful editors at Oxford University Press. They put up with a lot, not the least of which was my continual request to substitute my "new and improved" version of the manuscript for the "new and improved version" of the previous day (despite all my "promises" to cease and desist from unending textual emendations)! While on the topic of "putting up", great appreciation goes to my wife, Judith Loftus, and my children, Nate and Eli, who had to endure a husband and father whose odd behaviors reached new levels as a result of my obsession with this project.

Finally, I want to stress that all of these individuals deserve credit for making my book better than it otherwise would have been. Any obscurities, weak arguments, and incoherencies that remain do so despite their best efforts to set me on the correct path.

THE TWO SELVES

Chapter 1

Introductory Remarks about the Problem of the Self

The "self" is perhaps the most familiar yet elusive aspect of human experience. As a concept, it has captured the imagination of investigators and theoreticians from a diverse array of academic disciplines and cultural traditions (for reviews, see Albahari, 2006; Chadha, 2013; Dainton, 2008; Eakins, 2008; Ganeri, 2012; Gergen, 1971; Ismael, 2007; Klein & Gangi, 2010; Kircher & David, 2003; Leary & Tagney, 2012; Leahy, 1985; Legrand & Ruby, 2009; Lund, 2005; Mischel, 1977; Sedikides & Spencer, 2007; Siderits, 2003; Stern, 1985; Strauss & Goethals, 1991; Strawson, 2009; Symonds, 1951; Yao, 2005). But to what does the term "self" refer? What is a self?[1]

As psychologists and philosophers have made abundantly clear, the answer is elusive at best. Klein and Gangi (2010; Klein, 2010) have proposed that Bertrand Russell's (1912/1999; 1913/1992; see also Gendlin, 1962) distinction between knowledge by acquaintance and knowledge by description provides a perspective on the source of conflict between our everyday experience of self and our capacity (or lack thereof) to convincingly capture our experience in descriptive, theoretical terms. Russell, in his classic work, proposed we have knowledge by acquaintance when we know something via direct personal contact (sensory or introspective) and exhibit that knowledge by using appropriately referential terms when we communicate with others.

With respect to the self, this is seen in the ease with which we talk about the self as well as understand talk about self by others. However, when we attempt to make explicit what it is we refer to— i.e., when we are asked to describe what the word "self" means— problems quickly arise. Despite centuries of thought devoted to the problem, it has proven notoriously difficult to provide a set of propositions capable of transforming our acquired knowledge into a satisfying description of what a self *is* (see, e.g., Klein, 2010).

Indeed, some have argued that the question is based on the illusion that there is an elusive self to be explained (see, e.g., Dennett, 1991; Hood, 2012; Hume, 1739–1740/1978[2]; Metzinger, 2009; Pessoa, Thompson, & Noe, 1998; for a critical discussion, see Siderits, Thompson, & Zahavi, 2011). In this view, there is no question in need of an answer. One problem with this view, however, is that an illusion is an experience, and an experience requires an experiencer (e.g., Klein, 2012a; in press-a; Schwerin, 2012; Strawson, 2011a; Zahavi, 2005). As Meixner (2008) puts it, "The fictionalization of subjects of experience is incoherent, since it involves the incoherent idea that I, for example, am an illusion of myself" (p. 162). Immanuel Kant (1998) goes even further, arguing that the self of subjective awareness (his "transcendental ego") *must* accompany experience (for related views, see James, 1890; Lund, 2005).

It thus seems impossible to deny that we are aware of our own existence as a subjective entity (Descartes, 1984). Even if some philosophers and psychologists treat the existence of self as a live question, we know from direct, first-person subjectivity (that is, acquaintance) that the experiences we have are real to us and uniquely our own (that is, we have a sense of personal ownership of our mental states).

Despite deep concerns about the metaphysical status of "the self," psychologists have devoted considerable time and effort putting the term to work in an abundance of *self*-hyphenated compounds (e.g., self-comparison, self-concept, self-deception, self-esteem, self-handicapping, self-image, self-perception, self-regulation, self-reference, self-verification; for review, see Kihlstrom, Cantor, Albright, Chew, Klein, & Niedenthal, 1988; Leary & Tagney, 2012). But what is it that is being verified, conceptualized, esteemed, deceived, verified, regulated, and handicapped? Unfortunately, the focus of research rests firmly on the entries on the right-hand side of the hyphenated relationship—to the detriment of our understanding of the self in terms of its properties and causal potencies (for discussion, see Klein, 2010, 2012a, 2012b; Klein & Gangi, 2010).[3]

These concerns do not mean that psychology has failed to propose models of the self. On the contrary, formalizations of self have been on display for more than 100 years (e.g., Calkins, 1915; Conway, 2005; Greenwald, 1981; James, 1890; Kihlstrom & Klein, 1994; Klein, 2004; Neisser, 1988; Samsonovich & Nadel, 2005; Stuss, 1991). Yet the elusive nature of the construct has resulted in most of these offerings concentrating on the task explicating the "self" in its assumed causal or foundational relationship to a specific set of predicates, processes, and contexts (cf. Leary & Tagney, 2012; Sedikides & Brewer, 2001). We thus find models of contextualized selves, cultural selves, social selves, cognitive selves, embodied selves, situational selves, autobiographical selves, relational selves, narrative selves, collective selves, etc. But consideration of what the self *is* that serves as the assumed bedrock for these cultural, social, cognitive, and narrative instantiations often is vastly under-specified (for discussion, see Klein & Gangi, 2010; Klein, 2010, 2012a).

Conceptual difficulties surrounding what the term "self" refers to are not restricted to psychology. These issues have been subject to intense debate in philosophy and theology (both Western and Eastern) for more than 2,500 years (for review, see Sorabji, 2006). The ongoing, multidisciplinary nature of these (often contentious) examinations of the self (for discussion, see Baillie, 1993; Chalmers, 1996; Flanagan, 2002; Gallagher & Sheer, 1999; Giles, 1997; Johnstone, 1970; Sidertis et al., 2011; Strawson, 2005; Vierkant, 2002) has left some wondering whether a conceptual understanding is possible in practice (e.g., Olson, 1999) or in principle (e.g., McGinn, 1991).

A STEP TOWARD A RESOLUTION?

One reason for difficulties faced when attempting to define or describe what we mean by the word "self" is that there is *not* a *single* self (see, e.g., Klein, 2001, 2004, 2010; Klein, Rozendal, & Cosmides, 2002; Klein, Cosmides, Tooby, & Chance, 2002; Legrand & Ruby, 2009; Neisser, 1988). Rather, careful analysis reveals that *two* ideas of the self are involved in almost every discussion of the topic, although these ideas are rarely separated. In this analysis—reviewed at length in Klein (2012a, 2012b)—the self can be meaningfully partitioned into two distinct, but normally interacting, aspects of reality—the epistemological self (i.e., the neurally instantiated systems of self-knowledge) and the ontological self (i.e., the self of first-person subjectivity).[4] These two aspects of self cannot be deduced from, or reduced to, a single, underlying principle, structure, process, substance, or system (e.g., Kant, 1998; Klein, 2012a, 2012b; Zahavi, 2005).

In this book I present theoretical considerations and empirical findings that, I believe, support the argument that these two types of self are metaphysically distinct aspects of reality. Accordingly, they are not reducible one to the other. Nor are they different ways of thinking about a single entity. One—the epistemological self—is a neuro-cognitive system of the psycho-physical person, and thus capable of being apprehended (and treated as an object). The other—the ontological self—is also a real phenomenon, but not a material entity; rather, it is the first-person subjectivity that apprehends the content provided by the epistemological self. As I will argue at some length, its status as subject rather than object means that the ontological self cannot be known by acts of perception or introspection.[5] Our acquaintance with the ontological self is a matter of feeling and sensing; it is not something that can be captured via descriptive analysis. Despite these differences in their metaphysical statuses, under normal circumstances the epistemological and ontological selves interact, and this interaction is a prerequisite for a subjective sense of self. Indeed, it is *only* via their interaction that a particular form of consciousness—self-awareness—becomes possible (these assertions are treated extensively in Klein, 2012a, in press-a).

GOALS OF THE BOOK

I turn first to what can be asserted with reasonable scientific warrant about the self. Specifically, I discuss what I call the *epistemological aspect* of self—the affective, cognitive, and neural systems (i.e., the psycho-physical or empirical self) assumed to be causally responsible for providing the ontological self (i.e., the conscious self of first-person experience) with knowledge of who and what it is. I do not address the question of whether a neuro-cognitive system must be capable of conscious apprehension to merit the designation "epistemological self," but my intuition is that what makes a particular system part of the epistemological self is the conscious apprehension of its offerings as "self-relevant" by the ontological self (e.g., Klein, 2013a). While this content certainly is a product, in large part, of unconscious neuro-cognitive activity, the epistemological self does not emerge as a distinct entity until that content is directly given to (Klein & Nichols, 2012) or inferred as (Klein, 2013a) self-relevant by the ontological self. In this sense I follow Fichte's doctrine that there is "no object without a subject and no subject without an object."

Following this general introduction, I focus on several of the sub-systems of the epistemological self, and present evidence both from clinically impaired and psychologically healthy individuals that makes a strong case for the functional independence of the systems of self-knowledge. A good deal is known about the epistemological self and its instantiation in the neuro-cognitive systems of the brain, and I will not attempt to reproduce these findings in their fullness. Instead, I refer the interested reader to recent, comprehensive treatments (Klein, 2012a, 2012b; Klein & Gangi, 2010; Klein & Lax, 2010; Martinelli, Anssens, Sperduti, & Piolino, 2012; Picard et al., 2013; Prebble, Addis, & Tippett, in press; Renoult, Davidson, Palombo, Moscovitch, & Levine, 2012).

The ontological self is discussed next. The ontological self is the subject to whom an experience is addressed (i.e., the intrinsic addressee of an experience). I then draw attention to the logical error of conflating the self as the subject of experience (i.e., an object) with the self as the agent of experience (i.e., a subject; for detailed treatments, see Earle, 1972; Gallagher & Zahavi, 2008; James, 1890; Klein, 2012a; 2012b; Zahavi, 2005). Finally, I examine the legitimacy of standard philosophical and scientific arguments against the existence of the ontological self based on its designation as a conscious, immaterial entity. In the process, I address a variety of concerns, including, but not limited to, (a) what we can legitimately know about reality, (b) the nature of causality and its assumed closure under the physical, (c) the metaphysical status psychological reality, (d) the consequences of a materialist reduction of psychological experience, and (e) the use of introspective reports as empirical data.

My goal in this section of the book is *not* to "prove" that the ontological self is a non-material aspect of reality; rather, it is to keep open the door to the possibility that the materialist dogma that characterizes much of modern science does not warrant the conclusion that reality, in its fullness, must submit exclusively to analysis in terms of objective, material entities. In fact, the principles of relativity theory and quantum mechanics demonstrate reality is not in principle open to such closure.

Finally, I present evidence from a variety of clinical domains (e.g., prefrontal lobotomy, chronic pain, depersonalization, schizophrenia, anosognosia, neurological damage) that bear directly on the question of whether the treatment of the epistemological and ontological selves as metaphysically separable is a legitimate undertaking. I conclude that the available evidence—consisting largely in reports of patients suffering various impairments of a sense of personal ownership of their mental states—support my contention that the epistemological and ontological selves not only are both aspects of reality, but are also functionally independent aspects.

SOME NOTES ON KEY TERMS AND THEIR USE IN THIS BOOK

In this section I spell out the intended meaning of several terms that play a central role in the arguments presented in this book. My reasons for doing so are two-fold. First, each of these terms is sufficiently important to the ensuing discussion that explicit specification of my (perhaps idiosyncratic) conceptualizations seems warranted. Second, some of these terms have more than one colloquially accepted use (e.g., consciousness); accordingly, a precise, technically-grounded treatment of their meaning helps establish a common referential base. While not everyone will agree with my definitions, there should be little question of the meanings I intend.

The Ontological and Epistemological Selves

It might strike the reader that my use of the terms "epistemological" and "ontological" in reference to the self is a bit unclear. Such concern is defensible, particularly with regard to the epistemological self. In standard philosophical usage, "epistemology" refers to the process of knowledge acquisition. In this light, it might appear that such a term is better reserved for what I am labeling the "ontological self." However, as I use the term, "epistemological self" designates self-relevant content (primarily neuro-cognitive in nature), rather than a *process* of content-extraction.

The use of "ontological" to describe the self of first-person experience is reflective of my personal belief that in cutting up the "self-cake" into two separate aspects—the epistemological and ontological—the latter is the essential part (if I only had a brain and no conscious life, I would not exist; if I had no epistemological self, I *might* still exist as subjective awareness—e.g., see the section

THE PROBLEM OF THE SELF

on decorticate individuals in Chapter 5). The conscious aspect of "mind" constitutes our initial and most direct acquaintance with reality—all else entails inference (e.g., Berkeley, 1710/2003; Eddington, 1929). If the reader thinks my ontological priorities seem heavily influenced by Eastern contemplative traditions (e.g., Albahari, 2006; Ganeri, 2012; Loy, 1988; Valera, Thompson, & Rosch, 1993; Yao, 2005), the reader would be correct.

A second reason I adopt the term "ontological" with regard to the immaterial aspect of self is to place it in sharp contrast with the widespread attitude among scientists and Western philosophers that the notion of a "subject of experience" is not to be accorded an ontological status. In this book I hope to show that this conceit lacks warrant, both scientifically and logically.

However, nothing substantive rides on my use of the terms *ontological* and *epistemological* as designators for the two categories of self examined herein. If the reader finds it helpful, she or he may think of the epistemological and ontological selves, respectively, in terms of dichotomies such as "self as object and self as subject," "self as known and self as knower," "self as experienced and self as experiencer," "the self of science and the self of experience," etc. (while most psychologists trace such distinctions back to William James, 1890, examination of the literature shows these ways of dividing up the "conceptual pie" predate James by at least one thousand years; Sorbaji, 2006). When the terms "epistemology" and "ontology" are employed without specific reference to the self, they are to be understood according to standard philosophical usage.

Consciousness

Consciousness is a topic whose explication (much less existence) has captured the attention of the most dedicated and able thinkers for thousands of years. Despite the optimistic claims of some (e.g., emergent materialists), continuing struggles with this topic show little evidence of any imminent resolution.

Analysis of "consciousness" has impressed upon investigators the need to partition the term into a variety of types and sub-types— e.g., access consciousness, phenomenal consciousness, state consciousness, primary consciousness, temporal consciousness, core consciousness, reflective consciousness, primary consciousness, sentience, noetic awareness, autonoetic awareness, creature consciousness, higher-order thought, pure consciousness, self-awareness, etc. While I appreciate the conceptual utility of many of these designations, my use of the term "consciousness" in conjunction with the ontological self is to be understood exclusively as the self-aware form of consciousness (e.g., not as sentience more generally construed).

Reduction

A reductionist approach is characteristic of modern science. The idea is to analyze complex phenomena into their basic building blocks, with the goal of piecing together the parts to arrive at laws that predict how they function collectively at various levels of complexity. A reductive metaphysics typically is conjoined with two postulates: (a) that nature is a reflection of the underlying mathematical order of reality, and (b) that reality, in its entirety, is composed of material substances. With regard to the former postulate, Poincaré (1952) puts the matter bluntly "We can only ascend by mathematical induction, for from it alone can we learn something new" (p. 16). Galileo captured both postulates in his famous declaration that anything that does not involve the study of the quantifiable properties of material bodies does not deserve to be called a science. While I recognize that philosophers have proposed new and more sophisticated versions of the reductionist metaphysics, not all of which involve reduction in the ordinary sense—e.g., supervenience (with regard to the mind/body issue, the basic idea is that there can be no mental differences without simultaneous physical differences; see, e.g., Kim, 1998)—the case can be made that, among scientists, the more traditional notion of reduction still holds sway.

In this book I take issue with reduction as a metaphysical commitment to understanding reality. I will argue that not all aspects of reality can or should be restricted or reduced to quantifiable, physical facts. Adopting the idealized formalizations of mathematical physics as a model for the study of human experience does not adequately capture the richness of human phenomenology (e.g., Koestler & Smythies, 1967; Valera et al., 1993; Wallace, 1993). However, I fully acknowledge the extraordinary success the reductive approach has enjoyed as a methodology. Accordingly, my concerns about reduction apply only to the former sense of the term—i.e., the assumption that a reductive analysis can capture reality in its completeness. When I use the term "reduction," it is in its metaphysical sense—i.e., the belief that reality must, of necessity, ultimately be amenable to analysis in terms of physical, numerically valued, fundamental constituents.

Entity and Aspect

When I use the term "entity," it comes with a specific metaphysical commitment. It is the aspect of reality that can be captured by terms such as "substance" and "object"—that is, things that are bearers of properties. It thus picks out aspects of reality that can be reasonably assumed to possess a material instantiation. The epistemological self is one such entity.

In contrast, the term "aspect" is noncommittal with regard to metaphysical status, admitting the immaterial as well as the material. The term takes no stance regarding whether its referent is "a bearer of properties." I will use this term when discussing the ontological self, although, given the term's inclusiveness, the epistemological self also can be taken as an aspect of reality. By contrast, the ontological self, in my reading of it as an immaterial aspect of reality, cannot be described as an entity.

Functional Independence

The contention that two systems are functionally independent does *not* mean that one has nothing to do with the other, or that they are *completely* separate. Rather, as Tulving (1983, p. 66) nicely puts it, functional independence means that "one system can operate independently of the other, though not necessarily as efficiently as it could with the support of the other intact system." In this book, I attempt to demonstrate that the epistemological and ontological selves are functionally independent in Tulving's sense.

Person and Self

"Person," as used in the text, is taken primarily in its forensic, Lockean (1689–1700/1975) sense to refer to a being with qualities such as thought, moral accountability, self-reflection, memory, and rationality. But these qualities alone do not make a person a person. Assuming that we have both immaterial aspects (e.g., souls), as well as material aspects (e.g., bodies), Locke viewed the concept of "person" as including an immaterial soul and an animal body. By this definition, "person" is not numerically identical with either the ontological or the epistemological self. Rather, these categories of self pick out different aspects of the person.

Material and Physical

The terms "material" and "physical," though very closely related, are not, technically speaking, two names for the same philosophical concept. However, as I use these terms, they are intended to designate the same thing—i.e., the aspect of reality that is identical with actually occurring states of energy and matter. Material entities (= substances = things) have properties, qualities, and dispositions and are known by those properties, qualities, and dispositions. I have little doubt that a more nuanced philosophical analysis would render my assumed terminological equivalence questionable, if not false. However, for my purposes, the terms "material" and "physical" are *sufficiently* similar that—despite damage this might do to hard-earned philosophical distinctions—they can and will be used synonymously.

Sense and Experience

In this book I describe the ontological self as something *sensed* rather than *known*. This might strike some as an odd comment. After all, is sensing not a type of experience and is experiencing not something we know about?

A few comments clearly are in order. First, my use of "sense" does not refer to conventional sensory experience. I make no strong claims about sense in this regard—that is, as the precondition for, and most often eventuating in, perceptual experience— though I very much doubt that when we "sense our self," we are having anything like a perceptual experience. Nor do I want to use "sense" to describe the experience of the content (e.g., memories, perceptions, fears, hungers, images, thoughts, etc.) of a mental state, content we can know about and, typically, describe. This is the type of experience James (1890) refers to as "thick." Third,

I think there are numerous different types of experience (experiences are by definition conscious and, as discussed above, there are variants of consciousness).

When I use "sense" (or sometimes "feeling") to describe our experiential acquaintance with the ontological self (i.e., the subject of experience), I am trying to convey a form, or aspect, of experience that is pre-reflectively felt "as myself"; that is, an experience taken *directly* without the need for inference or the need to refer to, acknowledge, or recognize the content of the experience. It cannot be thematized or otherwise analyzed; we are acquainted with it directly as a content-free feeling (i.e., a "thin" experience).

I must admit that I have no clever way of distinguishing these two aspects of experience (thick and thin), other than to say that, were we to canvass people on what counts as an experience (or at least as a *conscious* experience), they would probably have little trouble distinguishing their sense of personal existence (i.e., the ontological self) from their experience of such things as perceptual states, memories, emotions, beliefs, and so forth. Sadly, there simply are not words in the lexicon to capture the great variety of things we experience or the ways in which we are acquainted with those experiences.

Personal and Perspectival Ownership

In this book I draw heavily on the concept of the personal "ownership of one's mental states" and distinguish it from ownership of a perspectival nature. The difference between these two types of "ownership" is subtle and apt to lead to confusion. Though I take pains to explicate these different uses of "ownership" in Chapter 5, it will be helpful to address definitional issues in advance.

By "personal ownership," I mean that one's experiences are sensed or felt as belonging to the ontological self. Appropriation of an experience to the ontological self is pre-reflective, directly given as "mine." In James's (1890) expressive terms, personal ownership entails the feeling that one's occurrent experiences are imbued with a sense of warmth and intimacy.

Given the effortless and flawless manner in which this relationship between the content and ownership of an experience typically unfolds, we seldom are aware that there is a relationship being forged. However, as we will see in Chapter 5, in certain clinical conditions (e.g., depersonalization, thought insertion), the content of the epistemological self can be present *in* awareness, yet lack a sense of being owned *by* awareness. Under these admittedly odd circumstances, the normally invisible relationship between experienced content and the personal ownership of that content is made apparent by virtue of its absence. The content still can be known to be part of the self; but, since the connection between content and the ontological self no longer is pre-reflectively given, that knowledge is inferential (e.g., "the content is about me, it appears to be situated in my head," etc.) The afflicted individual may even be clear that he or she "authored" the experienced content, yet this knowledge does not, by itself, forge a directly given sense that "the content belongs to me" (e.g., Klein, 2013a; Lane, 2012). Rather, absent a sense of personal ownership, the experienced content is accompanied by a peculiar feeling of disconnectedness (Klein & Nichols, 2012).

Personal ownership thus serves as the "mental glue" that connects metaphysically divergent aspects of reality (material and immaterial) into a sense of oneness. Although this assertion begs the question by including the presumed function of personal ownership as part of its definition, I think the image evoked captures the nature of this form of ownership.

By contrast, perspectival ownership of one's mental states is not directly given as a pre-reflectively taken aspect of occurrent experience. Rather, it is characterized by inferential knowledge—the knowledge that one's mental states appear in a manner that is different from the way they appear to anyone else. While the content of experience is present in a distinctive manner (e.g., it is in my head), this does not, by itself, guarantee I have a sense of personal ownership of those states. (Readers may find this hard to accept. The automaticity of the "normal" relationship between content and experience—i.e., personal ownership—is our default mode of being. To truly appreciate the experience of perspectival ownership in the absence of personal ownership requires we actually undergo that experience [e.g., Nagel, 1974]. Hopefully the reader will never be in that position. The many clinical examples presented in Chapter 5 should help clarify my intended use of the term "personal ownership.")

What makes a state distinctly and uniquely "mine" is that I intuitively sense—without need for intuition, inference, or reflection—the connection between content in awareness and the *feeling* (not the *knowledge*) that this content is uniquely and infallibly my own (for more detailed discussions, see Albahari, 2006; Klein, 2012a, 2013a; Zahavi, 2011).

Immateriality

In this book I take issue with the metaphysical assumption held by much of Western philosophy and science that reality, in its fullness, is exhaustively captured by a materialist ethic. I argue that some aspects of reality may best be construed as lacking materiality. The terminological alternative to materiality I adopt is *immateriality.* Some readers may find this word too strong—suggesting a binary distinction between the material and the immaterial; that reality can be meaningfully apportioned into two mutually exclusive and metaphysically exhaustive aspects.

To those who feel I have overstepped the bounds of metaphysical warrant, feel free to substitute *amateriality* for immateriality. Though, as my spell-check function informs me, this is not an actual word (of course, as the reader will see, I often ignore the spell-checker's advice when I feel it in my interests to do so), it carries no metaphysical commitments other than the idea that some aspects of reality are simply "not material." Immateriality, in contrast, can be taken as implying that reality lacking a material aspect *is,* by default, immaterial. This is something I believe to be the case, but I cannot possibly know to be true (see Chapter 3 for reasons for my inability to state with certainty what the non-material aspects of reality entail). Accordingly, *amateriality* has the advantage of metaphysical caution, stipulating what is *not* the case, rather than what *is* the case.

EPISODIC AND SEMANTIC LONG TERM MEMORY

Psychologists generally agree that long term memory stores two basic types of information, procedural and declarative (e.g., Klein, 2004, 2013a; Parkin, 1993; Schacter & Tulving, 1994; Tulving, 1983, 1995). Procedural memory makes possible the acquisition and retention of motor, perceptual and cognitive skills (e.g., knowing how to ride a bike; knowing how to read a line of text); it consists in the expression of previously acquired behavioral skills and cognitive procedures (e.g., Parkin, 1993; Tulving, 1985; Tulving & Schacter, 1990).

Declarative memory, by contrast, consists in facts and beliefs about the world (e.g., knowing that canaries are yellow; knowing that I ate lunch with my wife on Saturday at our favorite cafe). Conceptually, the difference between procedural and declarative memory coincides with Ryle's (1949) classic distinction between *knowing how* (operating on the environment in ways difficult to verbalize) and *knowing that* (stating knowledge in the form of propositions).

Tulving (1983, 1985, 1993) distinguishes two types of declarative memory: episodic and semantic (see also Cermak, 1984; Dere, Easton, Nadel, & Huston, 2008; Parkin, 1993). Semantic memory is considered to be generic, context-free knowledge about the world, such as *Bananas are edible, 2 + 2 = 4* and *Hartford is the capital of Connecticut*. Semantic memory is context-free in the sense that, when experienced, it is present in awareness as occurrent knowledge without regard to where and when that knowledge was obtained (e.g., Klein, 2013a, 2013b; Perner & Ruffman, 1994; Tulving 1983, 1993, 1995; Wheeler, Stuss, & Tulving, 1997). Although semantic memories often make no reference to the self or one's past (e.g., *dog's are mammals; bananas are edible*), semantic content can consist in propositions expressing facts about both the self and temporality (e.g., *Stan Klein was born in New York in 1952*), just as it can about other facts about the world (for review, see Klein, 2013b; Klein & Lax, 2010). But this information is known in the same way that one knows that bananas are edible; it is experienced as occurrent rather than as recollected (i.e., the content of semantic memory is felt to be part of current awareness rather than a re-living of the episode in which the content was acquired).

In contrast to semantic memory, episodic memory records events as having been experienced by the self at a particular point in time and space. When retrieved, these events are re-experienced (often in a quasi-perceptual way), accompanied by the awareness that "this happened to *me* in *my* past" (Tulving calls this awareness "autonoetic"; for discussion, see Klein, 2013a, 2013b; Suddendorf & Corballis, 1997; Tulving, 1985, 1993; Wheeler et al., 1997). Every episodic memory, by definition, entails a mental representation of the self as the agent or recipient of some action, or as the stimulus or experiencer of some state (e.g., James, 1890—though James did not use the term "episodic"; Klein, 2001, 2004; Tulving, 1983, 1995). Examples of episodic memory are *mentally re-living the experience of attending a concert last weekend* and *recollecting my meeting with Judith yesterday after class.*[6]

Chapter 2

The Epistemological Self—The Self of Neural Instantiation

THE EPISTEMOLOGICAL SELF—THE NEURO-COGNITIVE CATEGORIES OF SELF-KNOWLEDGE

It is a fact of scientific inquiry and personal experience that the epistemological self is able to learn about the individual in which it is situated (the classic psychological treatment is William James, 1890; more modern accounts can be found in Cassam, 1994; Gertler, 2011; Heartherton, 2007; Kihlstrom & Klein, 1994; Klein, Cosmides, Tooby, & Chance, 2002; Rosenthal, 1991; Wright, Smith, & Macdonald, 1998). Scientific discussions of the mechanisms that allow information about the self to be acquired, stored, and retrieved are on full display in academic psychology, even though thorny issues of *who* is doing the knowing and *how* this is accomplished remain largely unaddressed (see, e.g., Klein, 2004, 2012a, 2012b, in press-a).

Considerable scientific progress has been made on our understanding of the epistemological self. This is because, unlike the ontological self (as will be discussed in the Chapter 3), properties of the epistemological self—i.e., the neuro-cognitive bases of self-knowledge—are amenable to objectification and quantification, and thus are scientifically tractable. Not surprisingly, exploration of the social, cognitive, and neurological systems both contributing to and underlying our knowledge of who and what we are constitute the overwhelming majority of the more than 6,000 papers (Baressi, 2011) published since the self's legitimacy as an object of scientific investigation re-emerged following the decline of hard-line positivism's informal ban on "black box" psychology. While it is not the purpose of this book to review all of these findings, recent treatments can be found in Klein & Gangi (2010), Klein & Lax (2010), Martinelli, Sperduti, & Piolino (2012), and Prebble et al. (in press).

Studies of the epistemological self suggest that it is composed of a number of different, functionally isolatable neuro-cognitive systems (for reviews, see Klein, 2004; Klein & Gangi, 2010; Klein & Lax, 2010; Neisser, 1988; Prebble et al., in press). These include, but are *not* limited to:

1. Episodic memories of one's life events (see, e.g., Klein, 2001; Klein, Loftus, & Kihlstrom, 1996; Klein, Rozendal, & Cosmides, 2002; Stuss & Guzman, 1988: Young & Saver, 2001).
2. Semantic summaries of one's personality traits (see, e.g., Klein, 2004; Klein & Lax, 2010; Klein, Loftus, Trafton, & Fuhrman, 1992; Tulving, 1993).
3. Semantic knowledge of facts about one's life (see, e.g., Hurley, Maguire, & Vargha-Khadem, 2011; Klein, Rozendal, & Cosmides, 2002; Kopelman, Wilson, & Baddeley, 1989).
4. An experience of continuity through time: The "I" experienced now is connected to the "I" experienced at previous

(as well as later) points in one's life. Episodic memory is known to contribute heavily to this ability (see, e.g., Dalla Barba, 2001; Klein, Loftus, & Kihlstrom, 2002; Tulving, 1985), although semantic memory makes a contribution as well (see, e.g., Hurley, Maguire, & Vargha-Khadem, 2011; Irish, Addis, Hodges, & Piguet, 2012; Klein, 2013b; Klein, Loftus, & Kihlstrom, 2002).

5. The physical self: the ability to represent and recognize (e.g., in mirrors, photographs) one's body (see, e.g., Gallagher & Cole, 1995; Gillihan & Farah, 2005; Hehman, German, & Klein, 2005; Keenan, 2003; Klein, 2010; Olson, 1997, 2007).

6. The emotional self: the ability to experience and produce emotional states that provide value, affective valence, and evaluative direction to our actions and reasoning (see, e.g., Damasio, 1994, 1999; Mills, 1997, 1998; Singer & Salovey, 1993).[1]

While in normal individuals these sources of self-knowledge work together to help create our sense of self as a subjective unity (see, e.g., Damasio, 1999; White, 1990), taken individually, none of these systems is either necessary or sufficient to maintain the experience of the self as a singular, subjective point of view (Albahari, 2006; Klein, 2012a). For example, it has been shown that the first three sources of self-knowledge in the above list can be partially, or even completely, impaired without a corresponding loss in one's ability to experience the self as a singular, unique source of subjectivity (see, e.g., Albahari, 2006; Ganeri, 2012; Klein, 2012a). Indeed, the archives of neurology are filled with cases of individuals who lack access (in varying degrees) to self-constituting knowledge-bases, yet maintain a sense of personal identity and subjective unity (for relevant data and review, see Caddell & Clare, 2010; Eakin, 2008; Feinberg, 2009; Feinberg & Keenan, 2005; Kircher & David, 2003; Klein, 2001, 2004, 2010, 2012a, in press-a; Klein & Gangi, 2010; Legrand & Ruby, 2009; Rathbone, Moulin, & Conway, 2009; Zahavi, 2005).

MAKING THE CASE FOR THE SCIENTIFIC TRACTABILITY AND FUNCTIONAL INDEPENDENCE OF COMPONENTS OF THE EPISTEMOLOGICAL SELF

In what follows, I focus on evidence for the empirical treatment and functional independence of the first three components of the epistemological self. The research I present demonstrates that episodic-based self-narratives, trait self-knowledge, and personal semantic facts are all amenable to scientific analysis, and that such analysis provides good reasons to take these systems as functionally independent—though normally interacting—components of the epistemological self. I will not discuss the evidence for the final three components of the epistemological self (i.e., temporal, physical, and emotional), as far less research has specifically been devoted to their role as "systems" of self. However, the interested reader can find reasonably comprehensive treatment in Klein, German, Cosmides, & Gabriel, (2004), Klein, Gabriel, Gangi, & Robertson, (2008) and Hehman, German, & Klein (2005).

My investigations of the first three systems of the epistemological self began with a very simple question: "How does a person know that he or she possesses some traits but not others?" At the time, two views were current in the literature: the semantic abstraction view and the episodic computational view (summarized in

Klein & Loftus, 1993a). The abstraction view maintained that information about one's personality traits is abstracted primarily (though not exclusively; see, e.g., Klein, Sherman, & Loftus, 1996) from specific behaviors, either as they happen or on the basis of episodic memories of these behaviors. These abstractions are stored in the form of pre-computed trait summaries in semantic memory (see, e.g., Buss & Craik, 1983; Klein & Loftus, 1993a; Klein, Loftus, Trafton, & Fuhrman, 1992; Klein & Sherman, 1994; Lord, 1993; Sherman, 1996). Trait judgements are made by direct retrieval from this semantic store. When a trait summary is retrieved, trait-consistent episodes are not retrieved along with it (because the information they provide would be redundant; see, e.g., Klein, Cosmides, Tooby, & Chance, 2002). Trait-consistent episodes are consulted only when retrieval mechanisms fail to access trait summaries (e.g., when a summary does not exist yet for a particular trait; see Klein & Loftus, 1993a, 1993b; Klein, Loftus, Trafton, & Fuhrman, 1992).

The computational view, in contrast, assumed there is a mechanism that makes trait judgements online by retrieving trait-relevant behaviors from episodic memory and computing their similarity to the trait being judged (see, e.g., Bower & Gilligan, 1979; Keenan, 1993; Locksley & Lenauer, 1981; Smith & Zarate, 1992). For example, if I am asked whether I am friendly, this mechanism would search the episodic memory store for trait-consistent episodes (i.e., records of events in which my behavior was friendly). A judgement then would be computed from the episodes retrieved (based, e.g., on how diagnostic they were of friendliness or on how fast they could be retrieved).

These views carry very different predictions about the need to access episodic memories when making trait judgements. If the computational view is correct, then trait-consistent episodes must be retrieved to make a trait judgement. If the abstraction view is correct, then trait-consistent episodes will not be retrieved in making a trait judgement, except under certain circumstances (e.g., the absence of a summary).

These predictions have been extensively tested through paradigms that take advantage of priming, encoding specificity, encoding variability, patients with specific memory impairments, and several other research techniques. The priming study results will be described below (for converging results using the other methods, see, e.g., Klein, Babey, & Sherman, 1997; Klein, Cosmides, Costabile, & Mei, 2002; Klein, Costabile, & Cosmides, 2003; Klein & Loftus, 1993a; Klein, Loftus, & Burton, 1989; Klein, Loftus, & Kihlstrom, 1996; Klein, Loftus, & Plog, 1992; Klein, Loftus, Trafton, & Fuhrman, 1992; Klein, Rozendal, & Cosmides, 2002).

Testing for Trait Summaries: The Priming Task and Neurologically Unimpaired Participants

In our priming studies, my colleagues and I presented each subject with many pairs of tasks (pair members were referred to as the "initial task" and the "target task" to highlight their temporal relationship). Each task pairing involved a particular trait adjective (e.g., *stubborn*). The initial task was the potential "prime." The time required to perform the target task served as the dependent variable. The independent variable was the nature of the initial task—that is, the prime.

In one version of the priming paradigm, the initial task was either a *describe* task or a *control* task (other versions are summarized in Klein & Loftus, 1993a). The *describe* task asked subjects to judge whether the trait adjective was self-descriptive (e.g., "Does this describe you: Stubborn?"). The control task varied depending on the experiment; sometimes it was a *define* task (e.g., "Think of the definition of the word stubborn"), sometimes it was a request simply to *read* the adjective presented. Control tasks were shown not to elicit retrieval of trait-relevant behavioral episodes (more about this later). The target task in this particular version of our priming studies was the *recall* task (e.g., "Think of a specific time in which you behaved in a stubborn manner"). In all of our studies we made sure to pair the task of interest (e.g., the *recall* target task) with several "dummy" target tasks (i.e., tasks that followed performance of the initial task but were unrelated to the *recall* task demands) so subjects would not be able to anticipate which target task they would be requested to perform (and therefore be unable to prepare their response in advance).

If the episodic computational view is correct, then trait-consistent episodes will be activated whenever one is asked to decide whether a trait describes oneself—e.g., by performing the *describe* task. If trait-consistent episodic memories are activated, then one should be able to retrieve those memories faster (e.g., during performance of a *recall* target task) after performing a *describe* task than after performing a *control* task.

This was not the case. When subjects were asked to recall a specific behavioral incident in which they manifested a particular trait (the *recall* target task), those who had initially performed a *describe* task were no faster than those who had not (see, e.g., Klein & Loftus, 1990, 1993a, 1993b; Klein et al., 1989; Klein, Loftus, Trafton, & Fuhrman, 1992; for a recent summary, see Klein, Robertson, Gangi, & Loftus, 2008). Yet the procedure has been shown to be sufficiently sensitive to detect episodic priming when it occurs (see, e.g., Babey, Queller, & Klein, 1998; Klein, Loftus, Trafton, & Fuhrman,

26

1992; Schell, Klein, & Babey, 1996; Sherman & Klein, 1994; Sherman, Klein, Laskey, & Wyer, 1998; for experiments showing that this result obtains regardless of how "central" a trait is to one's self-concept, see, Klein, Cosmides, Tooby, & Chance, 2001; Klein & Loftus, 1990, 1993a; Klein, Loftus, Trafton, & Fuhrman, 1992).

Adequacy of the Definition Control Task

The fact that making a trait judgement did not prime episodic memories of trait-consistent behaviors is consistent with the semantic abstraction view. There is, however, a potential problem with this conclusion. Since the findings described are null, two possible interpretations of the data come to mind (see, e.g., Greenwald, 1975). First, the failure to find priming may indicate a functional independence between semantic and episodic trait self-knowledge. Second, it may simply reflect limitations in the method—e.g., the choice of the definition control task. Such concerns were raised early on about our research by both Brown (1993) and Keenan (1993). My colleagues and I subsequently have examined these alternatives, and our findings consistently support the first alternative.

First, a little history: Motivating our choice of definition-generation as our control task was the assumption that its performance would not involve activation of self-knowledge. Our assumption was based, in part, on the finding that definition-generation successfully had been used as a control task in many self-reference effect studies (for review, see Klein & Kihlstrom, 1986; Symons & Johnson, 1997). If definition-generation entailed self-referential processing, a define task should prove comparable to self tasks in its ability to promote good recall. Since this almost never happens—and when it does (see, e.g., Klein & Kihlstrom, 1986) the reasons are due to specific, theory-based, manipulations of the self-task—definition-generation seemed an appropriate control task to use in our priming studies.

Although the reasoning seemed plausible, we did not, at least initially, have direct evidence in support of our assumption about the lack of involvement of self-referential processing during word-definition. Fortunately, the situation soon changed. In 1992, my colleagues and I (Klein, Loftus, Trafton, & Fuhrman, 1992; see also Klein & Loftus, 1993a), demonstrated that, consistent with findings reported elsewhere (see, e.g., Ganellen & Carver, 1985; Kuiper, 1981; Markus, 1977; Klein, Loftus, & Burton, 1989), trait self-descriptiveness had reliable effects on the time required to perform initial (i.e., non-primed) tasks involving trait knowledge of self (e.g., the *describe* and the *recall* tasks). In contrast, *define* initial task latencies showed no effect of trait self-descriptiveness. If definition-generation automatically activates behavioral self-knowledge, and if the time to activate that knowledge is known to vary reliably as a function of its target descriptiveness (e.g., highly self-descriptive, moderately self-descriptive, not self-descriptive), it is hard to explain the absence of differential facilitation as a function of trait self-descriptiveness in the *define* initial task condition (for discussion, see Klein & Loftus, 1993c).

In other studies, we have used different control tasks and obtained the same results as studies employing the *define* task. For example, my colleagues and I(Klein, Babey, & Sherman, 1997) replaced the definition-generation with a task that required participants only to silently read the trait word presented. The *read* task functioned identically to the *define* control task.

Converging Evidence for a Functional Independence: Tests with Neurologically Unimpaired Participants

A considerable proportion of our published work on trait self-judgements has been devoted to explicating conditions under which priming will and will not be found. Specifically, we do not maintain that episodic and semantic trait knowledge are totally separate, non-interacting systems. Rather, we assumed the relationship was one of functional independence. Our functional independence hypothesis was not based exclusively on findings from the priming paradigm. As we observed (Klein & Loftus, 1993a, p. 15), "the findings from any one paradigm are open to multiple interpretations and vulnerable to the charge that they reflect more the idiosyncrasies of the methodology used than the variables of interest." Accordingly, Loftus and I and our colleagues complimented our priming studies with results from studies using other methodologies.

For example, we (Klein, Loftus, & Plog 1992) made use of the phenomenon of transfer-appropriate processing (see, e.g., Roediger & Blaxton, 1987; Roediger, Weldon, & Challis, 1989) in a study of recognition memory for traits, to show that different processes are involved in accessing the two types of knowledge. We (Klein et al. 1989, Experiment 4) applied the principle of encoding variability (see, e.g., Bower, 1972; Martin, 1971) in a study of recall for traits, and found that the type of information made available when making trait judgements was different from that made available when retrieving trait-relevant behaviors. And we (Klein et al. 1997) presented evidence from Dunn and Kirsner's (1988) technique of reversed association to demonstrate that trait judgements and behavioral retrieval are mediated by functionally independent memory systems.

Converging Evidence for Functional Independence: Patients Suffering from Neurological Impairments

Approximately 20 years ago, Loftus and I (Klein & Loftus, 1993) proposed that the study of patients suffering amnesia might provide a particularly effective method for examining the respective contributions of episodic and semantic memory to self-knowledge. This is because amnesic patients often experience highly selective memory loss, typically displaying intact semantic memory with impaired access to episodic memory (see, e.g., Tulving, 1983). Amnesic patients therefore present a unique opportunity to test alternative models of self-knowledge: Tests of trait knowledge can be conducted in amnesic patients with reasonable assurance that episodic memory for trait-relevant behaviors (a condition of the computational model) is not involved.

If semantic memory contains a database of personality trait summaries, then an amnesic patient should be able to know what he or she is like, despite being unable to episodically recollect the particular experiences from which that knowledge was derived. There is now neuropsychological data from a number of patients from clinically diverse populations (e.g., amnesia, autism, Alzheimer's dementia, schizophrenia) that speak directly to the issue (and, as we will see, others) of how types of knowledge about oneself are acquired and represented in memory.

In what follows, I present data from five patients—W.J., K.C., D.B., K.R., and R.J. Analysis of their impairments provides strong insight into the relationships between the factual, trait, and narrative components of the epistemological self. (Note: While I focus on the study of individual cases, most of these findings subsequently have been found to be applicable to the clinical populations from which specific cases were selected; for review, see Klein & Gangi, 2010.)

W.J.

W.J. suffered a concussive blow to the head shortly after completing her first quarter in college. Interviews conducted shortly after her accident revealed that W.J. had forgotten much of what had happened during the preceding 12 months—a period of time that included her first quarter at college. To document her deficit in episodic memory, we (Klein, Loftus & Kihlstrom, 1996) used the autobiographical memory cueing task originated by Galton (1879) and subsequently popularized by Crovitz and Schiffman (1974). W.J. was asked to try to recall specific personal events related to cue words and to provide for each recollection as precise a date as possible. Initial testing revealed that she was unable to recollect personal events from the past year. Over the next month, however, her amnesia remitted, and when she was retested four weeks later, her performance had improved to the point that it was indistinguishable from that of neurologically healthy women who served as controls.

On two occasions—during her amnesia and after its resolution—W.J. was asked to provide personality ratings describing what she was like during her first quarter at college. While she was amnesic, W.J. was able to describe her personality; more importantly, the ratings she made during her amnesic period agreed with those she made afterward, as well as with independent raters who knew her at college. Thus, while W.J. was amnesic, she knew what she had been like in college, despite the fact that she could not episodically recollect any personal events or experiences from that time period.

Could W.J.'s judgements while amnesic be based on her continued access to episodic recollections of high school or earlier—periods not covered by her amnesia? This seems unlikely. W.J., like many freshmen, manifested reliably different personality traits in college than she did in high school. This is not surprising given the newfound personal independence associated with the individual's abrupt change from his or her role(s) in family life to the freedom of college life. Yet W.J.'s self-ratings during the amnesic period reflected her college personality to a reliably greater extent than they did her pre-college personality. This suggests that W.J.'s ratings were based on semantic knowledge of her personality during her time at college, not on recollections of episodes from pre-college experience.

K.C.

Although the case of W.J. supports the independence of semantic trait self-knowledge from episodic recollection, it might be argued that a partial overlap between her episodic knowledge of her pre-college self may have enabled her to provide a reliable and accurate account of her trait self-knowledge during her amnesic episode. Such an account, however, fails to provide a viable explanation of the pattern of intact trait self-knowledge manifested by our next patient, K.C.

Patient K.C. permanently lost his *entire* fund of episodic memory following a motorcycle accident (Tulving, 1985, 1993). He also underwent a marked personality change following the accident. Nevertheless, K.C. was able to describe his post-morbid personality with considerable accuracy (his mother's ratings served as the criterion). The fact that K.C. could accurately report his own personality traits supports the view that knowing oneself does not require retrieval of episodic memories. It is consistent with the hypothesis that self-referential personality information is stored independently from self-referential episodic memory, in the form of semantic trait summaries.

It is important to note that K.C.'s self-knowledge reflected his post-morbid personality, not his pre-morbid personality. This means that K.C. not only had access to semantic knowledge of his own personality traits, but he was also able to acquire new knowledge about his personality. Yet this updating occurred without his being able to episodically recollect any information about the behavioral events on which this updating presumably was based.

D.B.

The case of D.B. (like that of K.C.) shows that one can have accurate knowledge of one's own personality traits even with a total loss of episodic memory. Patient D.B. was a 79-year-old man who became profoundly amnesic as a result of anoxia following cardiac arrest (Klein, Rozendale, & Cosmides, 2002). Both informal questioning and psychological testing revealed that D.B. was unable to recollect a single thing he had ever done or experienced from any period of his life. In addition to his dense retrograde episodic amnesia, he also suffered from severe anterograde episodic memory impairment, rendering him incapable of recollecting events that had transpired only minutes earlier.

To test D.B.'s semantic self-knowledge, we asked him on two occasions (separated by several weeks) to judge a list of personality traits for self-descriptiveness. We also asked D.B.'s daughter (with whom he lives) to rate D.B. on the same traits. Our findings revealed that D.B.'s ratings were both reliable and consistent with the way he is perceived by others (age-matched, neurologically healthy controls showed comparable correlations across sessions and raters). D.B. thus appears to have accurate and detailed knowledge about his personality despite the fact that he has no known conscious access to any specific actions or experiences on which that knowledge was based.

Thus, like W.J. and K.C., D.B. manifests a clear dissociation between episodic and semantic trait self-knowledge. But can semantic knowledge of one's own personality traits dissociate from other types of semantic knowledge as well (personal and non-personal)? Further testing of D.B. suggested that it can.

D.B.'s semantic memory also was affected by his illness, although this impairment was far less severe than that affecting his episodic memory (see, e.g., Klein, Rozendale, & Cosmides, 2002). For example, although he knew a variety of general facts about his life, he showed a number of striking gaps: He knew the name of the high school he attended and where he was born, but he could not recall the names of any friends from his childhood, or the year of his birth. He also showed spotty knowledge of facts in the public domain. For example, although he was able to accurately recount a number of details about certain historical events (e.g., the Civil War), his knowledge of other historical facts was seriously compromised (e.g., he claimed that America was discovered by the British in 1812, suggesting that he either has impaired semantic memory or that he is a revisionist historian!). Despite these impairments in D.B.'s semantic knowledge, testing revealed that his ability to accurately and reliably describe his personality traits was virtually identical to that of normal, age-matched controls. This result suggests a dissociation *within* semantic memory between (a) general semantic knowledge and semantic knowledge of one's personality traits, and (b) the intact ability to know oneself in terms of one's personality dispositions while suffering partial impairment of access to factual semantic self-knowledge.

Testing revealed yet another dissociation: D.B.'s knowledge of his own personality traits was intact, but his knowledge of the traits of others was severely impacted by his anoxic episode. For example, he could not retrieve accurate knowledge of his daughter's personality traits. The correlation between D.B.'s ratings of his daughter and her self-ratings was not reliable, and was less than half that found between control parents' ratings of their child and the child's self-ratings. Thus, although D.B.'s ability to retrieve accurate knowledge of his own personality was intact—i.e., it was no different from that of age-matched, neurologically healthy controls—he had lost his ability to retrieve accurate personality information about his adult daughter.

In sum, D.B.'s case goes beyond the episodic/semantic distinction, by suggesting category-specific dissociations within semantic memory (see, e.g., Caramazza & Shelton, 1998). His ability to retrieve trait self-knowledge is intact; his ability to retrieve his daughter's traits is impaired; and his knowledge about the world at large (and specific facts about himself) is impaired. This pattern raises the possibility that the human cognitive architecture includes sub-systems in semantic memory that are functionally specialized for the storage and retrieval of factual as well as trait self-knowledge. Additional data relevant to this claim comes from the case of K.R., below.

K.R.

K.R., a patient diagnosed with late-stage Alzheimer's dementia, shows that reliable, accurate knowledge of one's own personality can exist without the ability to update that knowledge (Klein, Cosmides, & Costabile, 2003; Hehman et al., 2005).

K.R.'s performance on standard tests of cognitive functioning (e.g., the Mini-Mental State Examination) indicated she suffers from late-stage dementia. She was disoriented for time and place and experienced difficulties with word-finding and object-naming. Her anterograde memory function was severely impaired, leaving her unable to recall events she had had in mind only moments before. Her episodic and semantic knowledge of her personal past was sketchy at best: for example, she sometimes believed her late husband was alive, and her estimates of how long she had lived in her current facility ranged from two months to 14 years!

Despite these profound deficits, K.R. had reliable knowledge of her own personality traits. We asked her on two separate occasions to judge a list of personality traits for self-descriptiveness. We also asked K.R.'s daughter and her caregiver at the assisted living facility to rate K.R. on the same traits. The results showed that K.R.'s test-retest ratings were highly reliable over time. However, her ratings did *not* agree with the ratings provided by either her daughter or her caregiver. This lack of consistency was not because the daughter and caregiver were poor judges of character; when asked to rate other individuals, their judgements correlated strongly with those of others.

How could K.R.'s ratings be so reliable, yet agree so little with those who knew her best? According to her family, K.R.'s personality and behavior had changed dramatically as the disease progressed, but she seemed unaware of her transformation (a situation fairly common among patients suffering Alzheimer's dementia; see, e.g., Mills, 1998; Seigler, Dawson, & Welsh, 1994). This suggests the possibility that the disease may have impaired K.R.'s ability to update the semantic records that store information about her personality. If her self-knowledge was intact but not being updated, then K.R.'s ratings may reflect her pre-morbid personality rather than her current one.

To test this hypothesis, we asked K.R.'s daughter to rate her mother on the same list of traits—only, this time, she was asked to base her ratings on her mother's personality prior to the onset of the disease. These ratings were strongly correlated with those provided by K.R. herself. So were pre-onset trait ratings of K.R. provided by her son-in-law. Taken together, these findings indicate that K.R.'s ratings are accurate, but reflect her pre-Alzheimer's personality.

K.R. also knows her daughter's personality traits. When asked to rate her daughter on the same list of traits, her ratings correlated strongly with her daughter's self-ratings. This is to be expected if K.R.'s fund of personality knowledge was created pre-morbidly and remains intact. But if, as hypothesized, K.R. had lost the ability to update her semantic personality files, then her ratings should be inaccurate for people whom she first met after the onset of her dementia.

This was found to be the case. On two occasions (weeks apart), K.R. was asked to rate her caregiver, whom she had been with for two and a half years. K.R.'s test-retest reliability was very low, in striking contrast to the considerable reliability evidenced in her self-ratings. Moreover, K.R.'s ratings of the caregiver did not overlap reliably with the caregiver's ratings of his own personality. This is not due to the caregiver's having a skewed view of himself: His self-ratings were strongly correlated with those provided by two age-matched, neurological healthy women living in the same facility, who had known the caregiver for about the same length of time. This also showed that K.R.'s inability to acquire new personality information was not a simple manifestation of the normal aging process. Clearly, the neurologically healthy age-matched controls were quite capable of acquiring accurate knowledge of the personality of someone they had recently met.

Thus, despite profound cognitive deficits, K.R. had intact knowledge of her own pre-morbid personality and that of her daughter. That her trait knowledge had been preserved and remained retrievable was remarkable, given the difficulties she had retrieving ordinary facts from semantic memory: such as the names of everyday objects, what a clock looks like, where she was, how long she had been at the assisted living facility. Like the case of D.B., K.R.'s preserved self-knowledge suggests a dissociation *within* semantic memory, indicating the presence of a functionally specialized database for the storage and retrieval of information about her personality (intact) and another database containing personally relevant factual self-knowledge (partially impaired).

It would appear, however, that the computational machinery responsible for updating personality knowledge (intact in K.C.) had been impaired in K.R. by the Alzheimer's disease. K.R. did not know her own current, post-morbid personality, nor had she been able to learn the personality traits of her primary caregiver.

R.J.

Patients K.C., W.J., and D.B. lost access to episodic memory as a result of brain trauma. However, there also are individuals whose episodic memory fails to develop in the first place (see, e.g., Ahern, Wood, & McBrien, 1998; Vargha-Khadem, Gadian, Watkins, Connelly, Van Paesschen, & Mishkin, 1997). Such developmental dissociations are particularly interesting because they permit inferences about the origins of self-knowledge that are not licensed by the discovery of dissociations caused by brain trauma and disease in adults.

Consider, for example, the hypothesis that semantic self-knowledge, despite being functionally independent of episodic memory, is initially constructed from a database of episodic memories. This hypothesis cannot be ruled out by cases like those of D.B., K.R., and W.J.: their intact semantic self-knowledge *could* have been derived from episodic memories acquired during the years prior to the brain trauma that caused their episodic loss as adults.

Now consider the implications of finding an individual who never has developed the ability to access episodic memories, yet has intact semantic self-knowledge. This developmental dissociation would suggest that building a semantic database of trait self-knowledge does not require access to a database of episodic memories.

Autism is a developmental disorder that has been hypothesized to impair the cognitive machinery that supports meta-representations from developing normally (see, e.g., Baron-Cohen, 1995; Leslie, 1987). It has been proposed that episodic memories are stored in and retrieved via meta-representations (see, e.g., Cosmides & Tooby, 2000). If so, then autism should disrupt the normal development of episodic memory. To test this prediction, my colleagues and I (Klein, Chan, & Loftus, 1999) assessed the episodic memory of R.J., a 21-year-old male with diagnosed with autism. Compared with ability-matched controls, R.J. was found to be severely impaired on a variety of tests of recall, especially when memory for personally experienced events was tested (by the Galton-Crovitz task). Although his impairment was developmental in origin, his episodic performance was similar to that found in cases of amnesia caused by brain trauma (see, e.g., Boucher & Bowler, 2008).

Despite his deficit in episodic retrieval, R.J. demonstrated reliable and accurate knowledge of his personality traits. His test-retest correlations were high and virtually identical to those supplied by matched controls. Moreover, the correlation between R.J.'s trait self-ratings and his mother's ratings of him was significant and hardly differed from similar ratings obtained from control mother–son pairs. R.J.'s self-ratings also were compared with ratings of R.J. obtained from one of his teachers; the correlations again were reliable and comparable to those obtained between control teacher–student pairs.

These findings suggest that R.J.'s knowledge of what he is like accurately reflects how he is perceived by people with whom he interacts. But how did he acquire this trait self-knowledge? His case suggests that access to a database of episodic memories is not necessary. R.J. cannot retrieve episodic memories now and, because his impairment is developmental in origin, he probably never developed this ability in the first place. All four previously described cases—W.J., D.B., K.C., and R.J.—show that trait self-knowledge can *exist* independently of episodic access; but R.J.'s developmental dissociation suggests that the *acquisition* of trait self-knowledge does not require episodic access (the same can be inferred for K.C.'s ability to update his knowledge of his personality).

As in the cases of K.R. and D.B., further tests of R.J. suggest content-specific dissociations within semantic memory. We (Klein, Cosmides, Costabile, & Mei, 2002) asked R.J. to judge features of common objects (e.g., "Is a lemon sour?" "Is a balloon round?"). R.J.'s answers were highly reliable across sessions. However, they did not correlate with those provided by others of the same mental age. There was high agreement among I.Q.-matched controls, with correlations among their answers ranging from .78 to .81. In contrast, correlations between R.J.'s answers and theirs ranged from .18 to .33.

R.J.'s atypical semantic knowledge is not due to a general inability to understand or answer questions—his ability to answer questions is fine, and when he is unsure what a term means, he requests clarification. This pattern—consensually accurate personality knowledge co-existing with odd, non-consensual knowledge of foods, animals, and objects—is thus surprising. One would think that the evidence of one's senses would allow the easy acquisition of knowledge about tastes, shapes, and colors. Indeed, words like *sweet, tall,* and *large* are more concrete and have more obvious referents than personality terms such as *kind, friendly,* and *ungrateful.* Nevertheless an individual with autism was able to learn his own personality traits, but was unable to acquire consensually held knowledge of foods, animals, and objects.

It has been proposed that culturally shared knowledge results when domain-specific inference systems interact with linguistically transmitted information, which the hearer stores—at least temporarily—in meta-representations (see, e.g., Sperber & Wilson, 1995). Deciding which part of the message is relevant requires one to make inferences about the speaker's background beliefs and communicative intent—which also depends on meta-representations (Cosmides & Tooby, 2000). This proposal could explain why a person with autism—whose ability to form meta-representations is likely to be limited—would have difficulty figuring out which knowledge is shared by those around him. Lacking normal meta-representational abilities, R.J. would have difficulty inferring a speaker's beliefs and communicative intent (see, e.g., Baron-Cohen, 1995). Without being able to store people's utterances in meta-representations, apart from semantic memory, he would take everything said to him at face value: other people's false beliefs, lies, ironic remarks, and metaphors would be stored in semantic memory as if they were true. Eventually, this could have the effect of partially corrupting his database of world knowledge (see, e.g., Leslie, 1987).

More recently, my colleagues and I (Klein, Cosmides, Murray, & Tooby 2004) found that R.J. failed to accurately differentiate between the personalities of his various family members, and that his ratings of them were less nuanced and less situationally specific than his ratings of his own personality. Specifically, despite the finding that R.J. had reliable and valid knowledge of his own personality traits (Klein et al., 1999), his ratings of other people (e.g., his mother, father, brother) failed to accurately distinguish among their quite different personalities. Rather, he viewed them all as essentially the same (the range of the correlations was .75 to .89)—in fact, R.J. gave his mother, father, and brother identical personality ratings on almost two-thirds of the traits he rated. This is not because his family members all shared the same personality profiles: The correlations they provided for each other clearly indicated that they saw themselves as reliably different.

Moreover, it is not the case that R.J.'s ratings of his parents correlated highly because they presented a uniform personality when interacting with him—R.J. also saw his brother as very similar to his parents. Nor is R.J.'s failure to distinguish among family members a side effect of his mental age. T.M., a cognitively normal male of approximately the same mental age as R.J., distinguished between his parents, yet R.J. did not. Evidence presented in the case study also revealed that R.J.'s high correlations among family members were not due to a tendency to assign a socially desirable rating to everyone (Klein, Cosmides, Murray, & Tooby, 2004).

Interestingly, R.J. was far more likely to assign extreme trait ratings—"definitely" or "not at all"—to family members than were appropriately matched control raters (the scale values were 1 = "not at all," 2 = "somewhat," 3 = "often," and 4 = "definitely"). Yet, his response repertoire was not restricted to the use of extreme categories. In his ratings of his own personality traits R.J., often used the intermediate category "somewhat." Indeed, in this respect his self-ratings did not differ reliably from self-ratings of cognitively normal controls. Moreover, R.J. used the category "somewhat" far more often in rating himself than in his ratings of others.

A "somewhat" generous (or kind or lazy) person may be someone who is moderately generous (or kind or lazy) in every situation. However, given that most human behavior shows considerable sensitivity to context, a more likely explanation is that "somewhat" reflects the perception that the individual being rated is (say) generous in some situations but not in others. On this view, R.J.'s use of "somewhat" indexed the extent to which he perceived an individual's behavior as varying across situations. If this line of inference is correct, then R.J. understood that his own behavior varied with the situation, but he failed to see the same is true (at least to the same degree) with respect to other persons.

This interpretation fits well with what is known about autism and theory of mind. As a result of this developmental disorder, it is hypothesized that the computational machinery that supports meta-representation is impaired. As a consequence, people with autism have difficulty inferring other people's mental states, especially what others think, believe, and know (i.e., the epistemic mental states).

These findings suggest that a person with autism can act on his own knowledge, whether he is meta-aware of that knowledge or not. As a result, R.J. can be aware of the ways in which his behavior varies as a function of context (at least as he construes it). However, his inability to correctly infer what other people believe, think, and know may be a barrier to his understanding how others construe their situations. To see the situational contingencies in the behaviors of his mother, father, and brother, R.J. would have to be able to infer what each of them thinks is happening in the situations in which they find themselves, even when what they think differs from what R.J. thinks. Yet many autistic individuals are notoriously poor at such "false belief" tasks (Baron-Cohen, Leslie, & Frith, 1985).

Summing Up

The neuropsychological cases presented permit me to draw some conclusions about how the cognitive architecture of the epistemological self learns about facts, personality traits, and past episodes in the life of the individual in which it is situated—that is, how the epistemological self-knowledge is represented in its neural framework.

1. Learning personality traits does not require access to episodic memories. K.C. learned about his post-morbid personality despite having no ability to retrieve episodic memories. R.J. also knows his personality traits, yet he has great difficulty recollecting behavioral episodes from memory. Moreover, R.J.'s disorder is developmental in origin, suggesting that he has never been able to retrieve episodic memories.

2. Alzheimer's dementia can damage the mechanisms that allow one to learn about one's personality traits. Yet the inability to update trait self-knowledge need not interfere with the ability to retrieve information from an intact, pre-existing semantic store of trait summaries (K.R.).

3. Any dissociation between semantic domains—whether due to brain trauma (W.J., K.C., D.B.), neural disease (K.R.), or autism (R.J.)—suggests functionally isolable storage and retrieval systems. But finding a developmental dissociation in R.J. suggests a functionally isolable *acquisition* system. His semantic dissociation suggests that trait self-knowledge is acquired via learning mechanisms that are functionally distinct from those that cause the acquisition of knowledge about animals, objects, foods, and people.

4. All five cases—W.J., K.C., D.B., K.R., and R.J.—show that trait self-knowledge can exist independently of episodic access and may constitute a separate sub-system within semantic memory (R.J., K.R., D.B.).

5. Trait self-knowledge is functionally independent of trait knowledge about other persons (D.B., R.J.).

6. Of focal relevance to the goals of this section, the evidence presented offers strong support for the contention that trait self-knowledge, factual self-knowledge, and episodic self-knowledge are functionally independent systems within the epistemological self.

An additional finding—though tangential with respect to the aims of this book—is that trait self-knowledge appears particularly robust in the face of neuro-cognitive damage (Klein & Lax, 2010). Studies of individuals suffering from amnesia, attention-deficit hyperactivity disorder (ADHD), autism, prosopagnosia, and dementia reveal that while most components of the epistemo-logical self can be compromised by disabilities, an individual's trait self-knowledge remains highly resilient. Recent work has extended this remarkable, and currently inexplicable, resilience of trait self-knowledge to patients suffering from paranoid schizophrenia (Klein, Altinyazar, & Metz, 2013).

While the evidence I have presented has been mostly from case studies, almost every one of these findings subsequently has been shown to hold true for the populations from which the individual patients were selected (see, e.g., Clare, Whitaker, Nelis, Martyr, Markova, Roth, Woods, & Morris, in press; Duval, Desgranges, de la Sayette, Belliard, Eustache, & Piolino, 2012; Matinelli, Anssens, Sperduti, & Piolino, 2012; Mograbi, Brown, & Morris, 2009; Morris & Mograbi, 2013; Picard, Mayor-Dubois, Maeder, Kalenzaga, Abram, Duval, Eustache, Roulet-Perez, & Piolino, 2013; Rankin, Baldwin, Pace-Savitsky, Kramer, & Miller, 2005; Renoult, Davidson, Palombo, Moscovitch, & Levine, 2012). In short, there is now strong evidence attesting to the empirical reality of the proposed systems composing the epistemological self.

Chapter 3

The Ontological Self—The Self of First-Person Subjectivity

In contrast to the epistemological self, the ontological self—the self that consciously apprehends the content of the epistemological self—is poorly understood on scientific grounds (for a detailed discussion of what can and cannot be said about the ontological self, see Klein, 2012a). Researchers often sidestep this difficulty, relying on their readers' familiarity with the term "self" (i.e., the self of subjective experience), derived from years of knowledge of direct acquaintance via personal experience (see, e.g., Russell, 1912/1999), to confer a (false) sense of confidence that he or she knows what it is the author refers to. But the problem remains— considerable ambiguity arises when we try to explain what we are referring to when we talk about the *ontological self* (as discussed below, the term is not open to being grasped and labeled via scientific objectification and quantification).

Compounding the difficulty, researchers often fail to appreciate that the ontological self is *not* the explicit object of their experimental tasks. Logically it cannot be. Objectivity is predicated on the assumption that an object exists independently of any individual's awareness of it; that is, that it is something "other" than the self (see, e.g., Earle, 1955; Hanson, 1958, 1971; Margenau, 1950; Rescher, 1996). When objectivity is the stance adopted by the self to study itself, the self must, of logical necessity, be directed toward what is *not* self, but rather to some "other" that serves as the self's object. To study myself as an object, I must transform myself into an "other," that is, into a "not-self" (see, e.g., Earle, 1972; Husserl, 1964; Rossman, 1991; Zahavi, 2005). As philosopher Roderick Chisholm notes, "one is never aware of oneself…although we may apprehend things that are *pour-soi*, things that are manifested or presented to the self, we cannot apprehend the self to which, or to whom, they are manifested—we cannot apprehend the self as it is in itself, as it is *en-soi*.…And Russell has frequently said the self or subject is not 'empirically discoverable'" (Chisholm, 1969, p. 7).

Thus, the ontological self is not, and cannot, be an object for itself and still maintain its essence—its subjectivity (see, e.g., Earle, 1955; Husserl, 1964; Neuhouser, 1990; Rossman, 1991; Valera et al., 1993; Zahavi, 2005). The ontological self is a precondition for experience—i.e., that aspect of reality that apprehends both mental and physical happenings—but it is *not* thematized by the content of experience (see, e.g., Earle, 1972; Gallagher & Zahavi, 2008; Ganari, 2012; Kant, 1998; Klein, 2012a; Lund, 2005; Siderits et al., 2011; Strawson, 2005; Zahavi, 1999, 2005). In this respect, it shares affinity with Buddhist reflections on consciousness as "the light that cannot self-illuminate" or "the sword that cannot cut itself."

Nor is the ontological self something one can locate via inference. I do not posit myself, nor do I have to guess that I exist. My sense of "self" is not something I *need* to deduce, infer, or reconstruct (intentionally or unintentionally). Rather, I immediately sense my "self" as myself, as a unique subjectivity (see, e.g., Earle, 1972; Ganeri, 2012; Husserl, 1964; Krueger, 2011; Lecky, 1945; Lund, 2005; Persson, 2005; Strawson, 2009; Zahavi, 2005, 2011). While Descartes (1984) inferred from his "thought" that he therefore must exist (i.e., "I think, therefore I am"), I would argue that this may be a valid mode of reasoning with regard to the epistemological self, but not with regard to the ontological self. For the ontological aspect of self, the proper stance is one of direct, pre-reflective, first-person awareness: that is, "I am, therefore I am." This self-referential awareness is a bare particular— that is, it is the irreducible, non-composite phenomenological character of experience (see, e.g., Chisholm, 1969; Earle, 1956, 1972; Kant, 1998; Klein, 2012a; Lowe, 1996, 2008; Lund, 2005; Madell, 1984; Melnick, 2009; Neuhouser, 1990; Siderits, 2003; Yao, 2005).[1]

I would go even further and say that the ontological self does not *have* properties such as feelings and thoughts, but is rather the non-propertied awareness to which thought and feelings (supplied by the epistemological self) are given. And, lacking properties, it lacks both materiality and the capacity for change (see, e.g., Earle, 1956, 1972; Klein, 2012a; though the contents presented to awareness by the epistemological self exhibit considerable flux; e.g., Kant, 1998; Klein, 2012a; for discussions, see Bayne, 2010; Earle, 1956; Foster, 1991; Lowe, 2001, 2008).

Moreover, I am immediately aware of my feelings, beliefs, memories, knowledge, decisions, judgements, and acts (i.e., the psychological processes that constitute the epistemological self) as mine—that they belong to the ontological self (see, e.g., Klein & Nichols, 2012; Lane, 2012). The experience of one's psychological states cannot force itself, via some scientifically accepted mechanism of physical force, on the experiencer. It "simply" is given to self-awareness (although, as we will see, this "given-ness" can come undone in certain circumstances). As William James (1890) says "It seems as if the elementary psychic fact were not *thought* or *this thought* or *that thought*, but *my thought*, every thought being *owned*" (p. 226, emphasis in original).[2,3]

The idea that the ontological self may be a metaphysical simple (and thus lack properties) may be troubling to those who take the position that we can know about any *object* we have acquaintance with only by virtue of knowing its properties. I concur with this sentiment. However, as I hope to demonstrate in the following sections, the ontological self is not an object and thus cannot itself be directly apprehended or thematized (see, e.g., Kant, 1998). As a form of subjectivity, it is sensed rather than intellectually grasped. Indeed, given the arguments just presented, the ontological self cannot be treated as an object without forfeiting its essential nature: not being part of the material aspects of reality, it is not capable of objectification.

This does not imply, however, that it is of necessity opaque to experience. As I argue below, such a conclusion follows only from the vantage point of an exclusively materialist metaphysics. And, as I hope to show, there is room for doubt concerning the viability of an exclusively a materialist interpretation of reality. While a materialist hegemony does not fold as a result of these doubts, neither is it unequivocally supported. Rather, the door is left ajar to the possibility of aspects of reality that lie outside materialist tenets. And, as I discuss in the next section, if we broaden the criteria for what is real, issues such as causal closure under the physical and causal interaction across metaphysically separate levels of reality take on less urgency.

MIGHT THE ONTOLOGICAL SELF BE NON-MATERIAL?

In this section, I address the possibilities of (a) broadening the concept of reality to include aspects not (easily) amenable to the materialist doctrine of science, and (b) interaction between aspects of reality occupying metaphysically different levels. It is not my intention to offer a knock-down philosophical argument for amending the criteria for inclusion in "reality" to encompass non-material as well as material aspects. I cannot do so, and, as best as I can tell, neither can anyone else. Nor is it my goal to address all of the philosophical positions (and their variants [and *their* variants]) that might be marshaled in support of materialism, immaterialism, or both—e.g., materialism (radical, non-reductive, emergent [epistemological, ontological]), constructivism, supervenience (weak and strong), eliminativism, panpsychism, parallelism, idealism (solipsistic, absolute), phenomenalism, dualism (property, substance [Cartesian and non-Cartesian]), pluralism, etc. Treatment of these largely disjunct and exhaustive views of reality would take us far afield from the points I wish to make; and I seriously doubt—given the number of (mostly incompatible) philosophical formalizations that have been proposed—that any satisfactory resolution could reasonably be expected.

My goal is far more modest. I want only to argue for the *possibility* that reality, in its fullness, might encompass more than currently is acknowledged by the materialistic ethos of much of contemporary science. To attempt to do more would be an exercise in self-delusion.

Many investigators, swayed by the materialism (i.e., the metaphysical view that there is a solid physical reality behind the veil of appearances), and reductionism (see Chapter 1) of contemporary scientific thought, regard the ontological self with deep suspicion—arguing that, since it is a purely mental event, it cannot include any physical processes or parts. Accorded a nonphysical status, the materialistic postulates of modern science appear to rule out the possibility of the self's existence (see, e.g., Bunge, 2010; Churchland, 1986; Flanagan, 2002; Kim, 1998; Kirk, 2003; Melnyk, 2003; Metzinger, 2009; for critical analysis and discussion, see Antonietti, Corradini, & Lowe, 2008; Foster, 1991; Hasker, 1999; Green, Stuart, & Palmer, 2005; Koons & Bealer, 2010; Lovejoy, 1930; Martin, 2008; Meixner, 2008; Shommers, 1994; Swinburne, 2013).

Investigators who hold that the existence of selves is obviated by these considerations (see, e.g., eliminativists) often fail to appreciate that (a) the self is *not* a unitary construct, but rather a *multiplicity* of functionally independent, yet typically interacting, aspects of reality, and (b) while the ontological self is not an object (it is a form of consciousness—self-awareness), and thus *not* privy to anyone but itself, the neuro-cognitive systems composing the epistemological self *can* be objectified and quantified, and are thus subject to materialist reduction.

Other investigators appreciate that the content of self-knowledge requires an awareness capable of apprehending that content. However, wishing to avoid a homuncular regression, while still adhering to the dogma of reductive materialism, they presume that if an aspect of self is required to apprehend self-knowledge, it is an aspect that, like any material object, can be treated as "other" and thus located, grasped, and studied scientifically (see, e.g., Damasio, 1999; Edelman, 1989; Pressoa et al., 1998).

A popular version of this approach to situating the self in the material world is mind/body identity theory, given modern form by Place (1956). There is now a host of proposals describing how this identity might be achieved—including, but not limited to, reductive materialism, psycho-neural identity theory, emergent materialism, and promissory physicalism. They all trade heavily on the proposition that mind (and thus self) and body ultimately are identifiable with the activities and properties of matter and thus amenable in principle to materialist reduction.

These arguments go wrong from the start, however, in stipulating that there is a single, unitary self that serves as the object of their metaphysical assumptions. As I hope to show in the penultimate chapter of this book, the epistemological and ontological selves, while contingently related, are not conceptually reducible. They are functionally independent. Since it is the ontological self that is the target of materialist concerns of contemporary scientific thought, it is the ontological self and its relationship to science that I turn to next.

Modern Science and the Ontological Self

The esthetic ideas of unity and simplicity are presumably still the most intellectual motives for the materialist's urge to simplify and unify: to shove entities into categories they do not seem to belong to, to make them the same as entities they do seem to be different from, to eliminate them, if need be, altogether from the realm of being, although they plainly seem to exist—in one phrase: not to accept entities in the way they seem to be.... These ideas and measures, however, cannot, in reason, be a guiding light regarding the truth of mind if they run counter to phenomenological seeming (that is: to phenomenological seeming that is verifiable as being intersubjectively the same).

(Meixner, 2008, pp. 157–158)

Modern science is simultaneously inclusive and restrictive. It is inclusive in its belief that everything falls within its theoretical jurisdiction, but it restricts what it allows us to qualify as "everything" (see, e.g., Martin, 2008; Papa-Grimaldi, 1998). Put another way, modern science trades heavily on the assumptions that (a) those aspects of reality, as we currently understand them, are exhaustive of the whole (see, e.g., Jeans, 1943, 1981; Margenau, 1950; Planck, 1925/1993; Reichenbach, 1951), and (b) the laws and constants of physics are universal in their domain of application (see, e.g., Bohr, 1934, 1958; Dainton, 2001; Lange, 2002; Papa-Grimaldi, 1998; Poincaré, 1952; Trusted, 1991).

However, as Earle (1955) sees it,

> We have no way of surveying the whole of reality; we have only a formal idea of it on one hand, and an infinitesimally small assortment of unclear objects on the other.... we must in other words hold our theory in precisely that tension which represents our honest position; we don't know what the entire character of reality is, and we should not attempt to close our ignorance through impatience with the infinity of the absolute itself. (p. 89)

As we will see, Earle's cautionary message receives strong support from a somewhat ironic source—the laws and principles of modern science.

Although scientists assume that their laws and constants remain unchanged at all times and in all places (see, e.g., Poincaré, 1952; Spencer-Brown, 1957), contact with reality is, in fact, limited to what we can observe locally. "To extend that knowledge requires both an act of faith in the uniformity of nature and a compromise with truth, for knowledge has an inbuilt uncertainty to it [*e.g., Heisenberg's principle of indeterminacy*]" (Shallis, 1986, p. 32; words in italics mine). To maintain that materialism, physicalism, idealism, or any other monistic metaphysic exhausts the nature of reality is thus to substitute doctrine for demonstrable fact. Such a stance forecloses what we allow to stand as reality by presuming that we have license to assert that reality, in its entirety, can be captured by our current concepts, methods, and instruments of measurement (see, e.g., Eddington, 1958; Elvee, 1992; Feyerabend, 1979; Horst, 2007; Jeans, 1943, 1981; James, 1909/1996; Kitchener, 1988; Margenau, 1984; Martin, 2008; Papa-Grimaldi, 1998; Stove, 2001; Tallis, 2008; Trusted, 1999; Vaihinger, 1925; Van Inwagen, 2002). To declare that the self (or, more appropriately, the ontological self) cannot exist (except in a materialist incarnation, and thus does not exist) is a metaphysical conceit lying outside what can be operationally justified (see, e.g., Collins, 2008; Meixner, 2008; Nagel, 2012; Swinburne, 2013). As I argue below, there is more to reality than what we know or conjecture about.

What Can We Know About Psychological Reality via the Scientific Model?

The mind/body identity doctrine assumes that mental events ultimately can be shown to be reducible to the activities of a material brain. This view is endorsed by the vast majority of psychologists and neuroscientists, as well as by many (primarily Western) philosophers (for reviews and discussion, see Batthyany & Elitzur, 2006; Bennett & Hacker, 2003; Bickle, 2003; Kim, 1998, 2000; Kirk, 2003; Meixner, 2008; Melnyk, 2003; Northoff, 2004). However, limits to our ability to measure reality, and thus to what we can know about reality, constitute a serious drawback for advocates of the material reductionist agenda.

Consider, for example, the "light cone" of astrophysics—i.e., the surface describing the temporal evolution of a flash of light in Minkowski spacetime. Events transpiring outside the boundaries of the cone cannot, due to the finite speed of light, send a signal that would have time to reach an observer (living or mechanical) and influence it in *any* way. A galaxy at a given distance from earth is defined to lie within the "observable universe" if signals it emits can reach us at some time in the future. However, because of the universe's expansion following the Big Bang, there are likely to be galaxies whose signals can never reach us at any point in the future. Since it appears plausible that the galaxies within our observable universe represent only a fraction of the galaxies in the universe (see, e.g., Guth, 1981, 1997), there is a substantial domain of "reality" residing permanently beyond our powers to know. It therefore remains a live possibility that aspects of the universe are forever barred from incorporation into our inventory of what is real (see, e.g., Aczel, 2001; Penrose, 2005). Thus, our exploration and understanding of the physical parameters of the universe is, by the laws of science itself (specifically, the theory of relativity), necessarily incomplete.

Turning from large-scale indeterminacies to uncertainty occasioned by the very small, Heisenberg's demonstration of a "smallest length" dictates that nothing can be known about the properties or behavior of entities that occupy minute regions of space (10^{-13} cm; see, e.g., Heisenberg, 1958, 1979; Margenau, 1950). Similarly, the *Planck length* is the spatial interval within which the properties of entities cannot be measured to an accuracy of greater than $h/4\pi$ (i.e., $\Delta p\,\Delta q \leq h/4\pi$), where h is the Planck constant, and Δp and Δq are the measurement uncertainties associated with the location and momentum of an entity (e.g., Jeans, 1943; Planck, 1960/1993).

It might, of course, be countered that, while we cannot know with certainty the position and momentum of an isolated sub-atomic particle, we can, by the principle of wave/particle duality, attain the relevant knowledge by reliance on the wave equations that describe quantum reality. This knowledge, however, comes at a price. According to the Copenhagen interpretation of quantum theory, to employ this mode of knowing, we first must collapse the wave equation. This is achieved through an act of measurement. Measurement, in turn, requires an observer—an observational necessity dependent, in part, on the assumption that there is no observer-independent reality (see, e.g., Bohr, 1958; Schommers, 1994). The ironic upshot is that we have reintroduced conscious-ness (via observation) into reality as a consequence of our attempt to deconstruct an argument for opening the door to its possibility!

The above mentioned constraints on our ability to "know real-ity" follow from the basic structure of relativity theory and quan-tum theory. Regardless of whether they ultimately are shown to reflect epistemological limitations on the scope of our under-standing, or ontological limitations stemming from the funda-mental nature of reality, they warrant the conclusion that we have no way (at least at present) to detect what transpires in certain minute regions of space (e.g., to do so would require a measuring instrument shorter than the segment to be measured, and this is logically impossible) or at great distances from our earthbound reference points (which would require transmission of informa-tion at a speed exceeding that of light).

Lest the reader form the opinion that limits on our ability to know reality are restricted to the very small and the very large, s/ he should keep in mind several consequences and implications of the limiting factors just discussed. First, micro-level indeter-minacies of quantum theory are not restricted to the subatomic level: they also have significant consequences for what transpires at the human scale. To borrow an example from Swinburne (2013), imagine that one constructs a nuclear weapon in such a way that whether or not it detonates depends on whether a certain subatomic particle decays within some finite period. Or, to illustrate this point with a more psychologically relevant example, according to the reductionist account it is plausible that activities of subatomic particles might result in a feed-forward sequence of causation leading to feelings of hatred, which, in turn, can result in a fistfight or even a world war. The "take-home" message is that *all* phenomena, regardless of their physical dimensions, are, to varying degrees, subject to quantum uncertainty.

Second, significant constraints on our ability to comprehend or probe reality are imposed by the limitations of our sensory capacities and cognitive abilities (see, e.g., Eddington, 1958; McGinn, 1991; Trusted, 1999). Thus, there are not only limits on what can be known that are imposed from without (i.e., theoretical constraints on what can be measured); there are also limits deriving from within (i.e., constraints on our powers to perceive and conceptualize).

Third, the inability to situate an entity, aspect, or process within an existing theoretical system does not license its debarment from membership in "reality." For example, thousands of years ago, humans learned to produce glass from sand, despite lacking any plausible theoretical model of how such transformations were accomplished. If a credible theoretical explanation were a prerequisite for bestowing existence on a phenomenon, designation of glass as part of reality would have had to await developments in chemical theory taking place in the eighteenth century.

In sum, theoretical, perceptual, and conceptual considerations logically entail that we cannot observe, much less speak of, the behaviors, dispositions, and properties of aspects of reality falling within (or, in the case of the light cone, outside) the borders of these epistemological "black-boxes." At the macro-level, limitations of our measurement techniques are still considerably greater than those imposed by the theoretical considerations of quantum indeterminacy. However, as Niels Bohr (1934) notes, should we, at some point, achieve great technical accuracy in measurement, the quantum barrier would still stand in opposition to our ability to appreciate reality in its fullness. Trusted (1999) succinctly summarized the situation: "We have either to accept that there is something inherently indeterminate about the physical world or that our present concepts of matter are inadequate" (p. 147). In light of these considerations, it seems clear that the existential status of the ontological self too often is held hostage to the stipulations of nomologically unverifiable materialist assumptions (see, e.g., Klein, 2012a, 2012b; Eccles, 1994; Earle, 1972; Jeans, 1943; Margenau, 1984; van Fraasen, 2005; Stapp, 1993, 2011; Swinburne, 2013).

The Possibility of Causality and the Problem of Energy Conservation Among Metaphysically Distinct Selves

An oft-cited objection to mind/brain interaction is that it violates the principle of energy conservation (see, e.g., Collins, 2008; Eccles, 1994; Lowe, 2008; Margenau, 1984; Metzinger, 2009; Stapp, 2011). The materialist version of this interpretation of causality assumes that a physically existing entity with intrinsic properties acts on other entities to alter their properties. For one entity to influence another, they must be capable of exchanging energy. Since energy, according to the special theory of relativity, is a property of the material world (e.g., $E = MC^2$), any exchange between the ontological self (an assumed non-material aspect of reality) and the epistemological self (a material entity)—assuming that such an exchange could be permitted between two aspects of reality, only one of which clearly has the status of *entity*—it would result in a net increase in energy in the universe, thereby violating a fundamental law of physics: the conservation of energy.

Objections based on energy conservation are grounded in the assumption that *all* causal interactions result in energy exchange. This assumption, however, does not enjoy universal agreement (see, e.g., Aczel, 2001; Afriat, & Selleri, 1999; Bell, 1993; Collins, 2008; Einstein, Podolsky, & Rosen, 1935; Greenberger, Reiter, & Zelinger, 1999; Hume, 1748/2004; Loy, 1988; Swinburne, 2013). For example, some models of causal influence trade on the assumption that what is exchanged between things in interaction is not energy, but information (see, e.g., Aczel, 2001; Fields, 2012; von Baeyer, 2004). Informational models have broad application to problems of causality (for the classic discussion of issues surrounding causation, see David Hume, 1748/2004), including physical phenomena not easily explained via traditional notions of energy exchange (for example, an event that affects an object residing at a distance that would require faster-than-light transmission of the event's causal potencies; e.g., Einstein et al., 1935). I focus here on an example more apropos to our mind/body concerns—i.e., the assumption held by those who model causality on the principles of interaction between objects—of an approximate ("approximate": due to unexamined factors and the strong possibility of causal interactions taking place in an open system; e.g., Emmet, 1985; Lange, 2012) equivalence of energy exchanged *between* cause and effect (e.g., chemical reactions, Newtonian laws of motion).

Materialist thinkers often adopt a view of causation grounded in principles applicable to understanding the succession of events taking place between physical objects (such as one billiard ball striking another). In this view, physical events are caused by other physical events. This, in turn, opens the door to the physicalist assumption that causal interaction entails an exchange of energy, and that the energy exchanged remains "approximately" constant (or exactly constant in a system known to be closed). However, intentions, memories, perceptions, beliefs, and other mental states whose causal efficacy trades on the notion of *information exchange* have potencies not easily captured by physicalist principles—in particular, the assumption that the energy exchanged between parties in a causal interaction is conserved. As I hope to show with the following thought experiment, a mental event (accompanied by small physical changes) can eventuate in disproportionately large effects—effects of such magnitude that they appear to be in violation of the principles governing causal interaction among material aspects of reality.

Imagine a piece of paper on which is printed a short, insulting remark. In terms of energy requirements, one can consider such things as the work needed to produce the ink and paper, the physical act of writing, and the emission of photons reflected from the paper and ink. Whether *all* of these energetic factors constitute the causal potency of the remark is questionable. Certainly, however, photons reflected from the letter have clear relevance to its causal consequences. While this is not much energy, it is a measurable, physical quantity.

Now consider the potential effect(s). A sufficiently *nasty* remark directed at a sufficiently *sensitive* person can lead to a verbal rebuke, physical attack, or even, if the person is in a position of political influence, a full-scale war between nations. Next, consider the energetic imbalance between the photonic emissions (an ostensible cause) and the detonation of a nuclear device (i.e., a potential effect). It commonly is assumed by materialist models of causation that every event is determined by a sufficient cause; that is, to be in a causal relation, the cause should be *adequate* to its effect (Earle, 1955; Emmet, 1985; Martin, 2008). But any notion of adequacy taken *solely* in terms of the "balance of energy exchanged between entities" seems incomprehensible—i.e., a relatively modest quantity of reflected photons results in the detonation of a massive weapon.

What we appear to have is the following: (1) a number of black lines on a piece of white paper are combined to fashion set of objects (i.e., letters) that appear grouped into several clusters (i.e., words); (2) these clusters have no intrinsic *meaning*; and (3) they emit a small amount of energy in the form of reflected light. A person senses the reflected photons, *supplies meaning*, and *interprets* the information (which is not inherent in the objects) as *offensive*. This results in a cascade of causes and effects that eventuate, in a worst-case scenario, in the release of several million tons of nuclear energy. To maintain the principle of energy equivalence, one might attempt to concoct an explanation of "cause–effect iterations" that ratchet up to the desired level of energy on the causal side of the equation, but this would constitute a rather forced story (e.g., none of the potential physical causes—i.e., the black marks on the paper—easily accounts for the amount of energy released by the nuclear explosion).

So, can this cause–effect sequence be captured in terms of energy balance? I do not see any simple way to do so (save, perhaps, by positing an open system containing a host of possible, but probably unspecifiable, causally relevant events). It seems that a purely physical object with minimal energetics (black marks on white paper) has caused an event whose relation to the ostensible "cause" (i.e., the black marks) is not interpretable in purely energetic terms. What is missing from this analysis is the recognition that what is being causally exchanged between the letter (i.e., object) and the person (i.e., mind) entails a great deal more than just energy: it includes *understanding* that the physical markings are a potential source of information, *interpreting* the meanings the marking are intended (by the sender) to convey, and other mental acts. In short, *information, not energy,* appears to be the causally efficacious factor in this hypothetical scenario. But to see this requires that we acknowledge that concepts such as meaning, belief, expectation, feeling, and other mental states have causal potencies, albeit potencies that are informational rather than energetic. And how does one, should she or he be so inclined, quantify the energetic aspects of a belief, interpretation or other mental state (for discussion, see below)? There are some hints of the possibility of converting information into energy (e.g., Toyabe, Takahiro, Ueda, Muneyuki, & Sano, 2010), but they require one to transform information *into* a material correlate *prior to* affecting the conversion. This, in essence, is empirically begging the question.

Controversies surrounding the question of the need to posit energy conservation as a prerequisite for cause and effect have direct relevance to the question at hand. Many neuroscientists have proposed that interactions between the self and the brain can be localized in activity taking place in regions falling below the assumed micro-limits of epistemological resolution (such as events occurring *within* microtubules, or in the paracrystalline structure of the presynaptic vesicular grid; see, e.g., Beck & Eccles, 1992; Hamerhoff & Penrose, 1996; Penrose, 1989; Redman, 1990; for review, see Smith, 2003). If these ideas are conceptually plausible, laws of energy conservation no longer could be granted uncontested applicability, since the regions of assumed causal relevance would be subject to quantum indeterminacy (i.e., the activities taking place therein would, in principle, be unknowable; see, e.g., Beck, 2008; Collins, 2008; Eccles, 1994). Moreover, as Meixner (2005) notes, there is little, if any, empirical evidence for the applicability of conservation laws within brains. Accordingly, the universal applicability of such laws is an assumption of the physical sciences—not, as often presented, an experimentally defensible result.

Another attack on mind/brain relations, derived from concerns about causal interactions across metaphysical levels (e.g., aspect and entity), claims that if the ontological self exists, it does so as little more than an epiphenomenon (see, e.g., Flanagan, 2002; Metzinger, 2009; for critical discussion, see Hasker, 1999; Lovejoy, 1930; Stapp, 2011; Swinburne, 1997). This existential designation, not surprisingly, is dictated by materialist considerations. Since, by stipulation, a non-material aspect of reality can have no causal relations with the material world (the principle of causal closure under the physical), the ontological self is, by definitional fiat, stripped of its capacity to interact with the world of physical reality—in particular, the brain (and thus the epistemological self). This is, of course, is the modern version of Descartes' Dilemma (see, e.g., Almog, 2002).

Recent years have seen a number of challenges to the principle of causal closure (the interested reader is referred to Baker & Goetz, 2011; Beck, 2008; Collins, 2008; Lowe, 2008; Stapp, 1993, 2011; Swinburne, 2013). These arguments—considered in conjunction with previously mentioned epistemological limits on our ability to speak about interactions taking place between aspects of reality occupying particular regions of space—suggest that the applicability of constraints embodied in the principle of causal closure to the ontological self are far from settled (Collins, 2008; Eccles, 1994; Margenau, 1984; Stapp, 2011; Swinburne, 2013).

In summary, assumptions about the non-material metaphysical status of the ontological self are *neither* confirmed *nor* refuted by consideration of principles such as causal closure under the physical. While I am of the view that the materiality of the ontological self is, at best, questionable (see also Dainton, 2008; Foster, 1991; Hasker, 1999; Kant, 1998; Lowe, 2008; Lund, 2005; Klein, 2012a, 2012b; Siderits, 2003; Swinburne, 2013), no definitive answer either for or against this position currently is in hand. As I hope to have shown, however, a *strong* stance with respect to the ontological self's metaphysical status—be it material, immaterial, or epiphenomenal—is not warranted.[4]

REALITY AND THE ONTOLOGICAL SELF

The arguments just presented pertain more to what we *cannot* say than to what we *can* say about the ontological self. Nonetheless, as Danziger (2008) observes, "opening the windows to shed light on difficult topics is likely to bring advantages when compared to a life behind shutters, even if the view outside is somewhat limited and distorted" (p. 21). In the case of the ontological self, this distortion is traceable to more than just perceptual obfuscation. It derives also from conceptual presumptions and theoretical dogma that have been conjoined with a desire to situate, in somewhat Procrustean fashion, a fundamental aspect of human experience within the currently fashionable metaphysical dogma of contemporary Western science.[5]

A basic premise of this book is that not *all* aspects of reality can be captured via objective, quantifiable treatment of a materialist ontology. Nor is uncertainty about "what is" restricted to errors of measurement at the conceptually opaque boundaries of the very small and very large. Why should a line be drawn in the sand between the microcosm and the macrocosm? After all, the latter is, by reductionist logic, *simply* an extension of the former. And if subatomic particles are not, according to quantum ontology, "real things"—e.g., Heisenberg's principle (Heisenberg, 1958), wave/particle duality (Jeans, 1943; Margenau, 1950), loss of individuality at the subatomic level (see, e.g., Pesic, 2002), or, more generally, Copenhagen Complementarity (see, e.g., Heisenberg, 1958; Bohr, 1958; Trusted, 1999)—then everyday reality does not constitute "things" either. To paraphrase a saying attributed to Nagarjuna, "if the seed is not real, how then can the tree be real?"[6] Matter has lost its substance.

So what can we say about the ontological self from the perspective of scientific analysis? It certainly seems a poor candidate for such a treatment. Science is an enterprise predicated on understanding objects, processes, and their relations. It takes as its subject matter the world of publicly observable and physically measurable (both directly and indirectly; via mechanical device, physical record, or other indicators) objects and events (see, e.g., Bunge, 2010; Earle, 1955; Margenau, 1950; Reichenbach, 1942/1970; Rescher, 1997; Shommers, 1994). Since nothing can be an object for the ontological self unless it is "other" to the self, it follows that the ontological self cannot objectively apprehend itself as itself (see, e.g., Albahari, 2006; Earle, 1972; Foster, 1991; Klein, 2012a, 2012b; Loizou, 2000; Lund, 2005: Nagel, 1974; Zahavi, 2005; but see Strawson, 2009, for an opposing view). For the self of first-person subjectivity to become part of the world of science, it would have to forfeit its subjectivity. Scientific analysis thus has the unintended consequence of eliminating the entity under discussion—the ontological self—from the discussion.

Objectification, Quantification, and the Epistemological and Ontological Self

Human experience does not easily submit to objectification, and thus quantification (see, e.g., Mitchell, 1999). This often is taken as a tacit admission that experience forfeits its status as part of reality. As Stroud (2000) sees it, one goal of scientific naturalism is to separate "reality as it is independently of us from what is in one way or another dependent on us and so misleads us to what is really there" (p. 4; see also, Ladyman, 2002; Sellers, 1963). In this view, objectivity trumps subjectivity in deciding what is real.

The doctrine that "reality" is that which distinguishes what truly is the case from that which only appears to be so is thought by many to be both overly restrictive and without firm foundation (see, e.g., Berkeley, 1710/2003; Eccles, 1994; Elvee, 1992; Feyerabend, 1979; Margenau, 1984; McGinn, 1991; Papa-Grimaldi, 1998; Popper, 1994; Shommers, 1994; Stove, 2001; Tallis, 2008; Trusted, 1999; Swinburne, 2013; Wallace, 2003). Dewey (1958) nicely summarizes the tension between those who would restrict reality to what can be objectified and those who see no rational basis for banishing subjectivity from the realm of the real:

> Since thinkers claim to be concerned with knowledge of existence, rather than imagination, they have to make good the pretension to knowledge. Hence they transmute the imaginative perception of the stably good object into a definition and description of true reality in contrast with lower and specious

existence...they remove the actual existence of the very traits which generate philosophic reflection and which give point and bearing to its conclusions. (p. 53)

Reality, Dewey continues,

becomes what we wish it to be, after we have analyzed its defects and decided upon what would remove them; "reality" is what existence would be if our reasonably justified preferences were so completely established in nature as to exhaust and define its entire being...what is left over (and since trouble, struggle, conflict and error still empirically exist, something *is* left over), being excluded by definition from full reality is assigned a lower grade or order of being which is asserted to be metaphysically inferior; an order variously called illusion, mortal mind or the merely empirical against what truly is...empirically, we have two separate realms of being...a classificatory device has been introduced by which the two traits have been torn apart, one of them being labeled reality and the other appearance. (1958, p. 54; for similar views, see Bohm 1980; Meixner, 2008; Nagel, 2012; Spencer-Brown, 1957; Popper, 1994; Wallace, 2003)

Quantification of experience is particularly troublesome when experiences are of mental properties contributed by the epistemological self (that is, constituents of what James, 1890, termed the "spiritual self"; e.g., thoughts, memories, beliefs, jealousy, loves, hates, judgements of beauty and ugliness, euphoria, depression, etc.; Mitchell, 1999; Uttal, 2008). An attempt to capture the richness of such phenomena in a quantifiable format has the effect of the leaving them experientially barren.

This is not to say objectification and quantification of mental phenomena (for example, those tied to the empirical self) is impossible. It is not! For more than 150 years, research in psychology has attested to the fact that the content of intra-subjective experience can be subjected to empirical analysis, providing descriptions and conclusions that attain inter-subjective consensus. The phenomenological content of a mental state need not be arbitrary, ambiguous, or inexpressible. First-person experiences are reportable and thus subject to objectification and quantification. But, as I hope to show, something(s) essential are likely to get lost in the process.

A classic example is Ebbinghaus's (1885) attempt to bestow scientific respectability on the concept of human memory by reducing it to a level at which it could be submitted to objectification and quantification (e.g., the number of nonsense syllables retained after the passage of various time intervals). In so doing, the phenomenon was impoverished to such a degree that it no longer bore any clear resemblance to "remembering" as it is *experienced* (see, e.g., Bartlett, 1932). Quantification thus comes at the expense of the phenomenon. The reduction of memory to a set of numbers (something we still do—e.g., number of words recalled; duration of retention; confidence-judgement ratings, etc.) reduces the fullness of the original experience to the point where it is a shadow (and that is being generous) of the phenomenon under scrutiny (see, e.g., Arcaya, 1989; Casey, 1979; Danzinger, 2008; Gallagher & Zahavi, 2008).

Consider, for instance, the experience of pain. An attempt to scientifically legitimize the experience via its objectification (e.g., the firing of C-fibers) and its quantification (e.g., Likert scales) often entails the use of psychometric instruments on which to indicate (a) the type of pain (e.g., sharp, dull, burning), (b) the duration of the pain event, (c) pain intensity, (d) the overall level of discomfort, (e) pain frequency, etc. Yet a collection of such ratings fails to capture the richness of the experience by focusing only on the aspects the investigator deems worth quantifying (or possible to quantify in a scientifically satisfying manner), while ignoring others s/he has not considered (e.g., aspects of pain that, while not part of its operational definition, have a considerable part to play in the experience—such as personal concerns, attention to the passage of time, anticipation of the future, social considerations, despair, stoicism, etc.).

Just as Ebbinghaus's reduction of the richness of memorial experience to a more tractable set of numerical values precluded him from appreciating many of the very things that define memory experience (e.g., effort after meaning; feeling attachment to the past; mentally reliving an event; the emotionality associated with a recollection; anticipation of the future)—so the attempt to reduce the content of the experience of the ontological self to objects capable of being represented numerically has the effect of rendering their phenomenological complexity unrecognizable. As Zahavi (2012) puts it, "I consider an account of self which disregards the fundamental structures and features of our experiential life a non-starter" (p. 157).

Objectification is even more problematic when the ontological self is one's target. As discussed, when objectivity is the stance adopted by the ontological self to study itself, the ontological self must be directed toward what is not itself, but rather to some "other" that serves as its object. Thus, objectification of the ontological self (and subsequent quantification) is not a logically admissible operation.

Saving the Phenomena

Sometimes appearances need to be saved and savored for the insights they provide about reality. While human experience may ultimately prove to be grounded in events taking place at the atomic (and subatomic) level, it is hard to see how reducing appearance to the motion, shape, and size of its fundamental constituents can't help but strip the phenomenon of its experiential properties and, potentially (see the earlier section in this chapter titled "The Possibility of Causality and the Problem of Energy Conservation Among Metaphysically Distinct Selves"), its causal potencies. A belief may be in error, a perception may fail to faithfully represent an object present to the senses. But atomic particles do not, and cannot, make errors.

Discussing limitations of a reductive analysis designed to connect the level of neuro-biological events with events at the level of mental experience, Antonietti (2008) observes,

> While in the scientific study of physical realities it makes sense to move from appearance (e.g., water) to a "deeper" reality (e.g., the molecular structure of water—H_2o), where the mind is concerned it is not a question of going to a deeper reality, because the subjective appearance is the essence of the mind.... Painfulness is not a contingent property of pain, painfulness is the essence of pain; there is no appearance beyond the pain itself; I feel pain, the sensation of the pain is all I feel; it is a non-sense to say the (experience of) pain is actually a neural process. (2008, p. 52; parenthesis added)

It is "a non-sense" since, although we understand how the properties of water can be connected to, and understood in terms of, the properties of the individual atomic constituents and their interactions, we cannot understand how the *experience* of pain can be derived from, or conceived in terms of, the physical activity of neurons.

The self of subjective experience, even if deemed a "lower grade of being" (see, e.g., Dewey, 1958), still is undeniably a ubiquitous aspect of our existence (see, e.g., James, 1890; Kant, 1998; Klein, 2012a; Zahavi, 2005), a form of being (see, e.g., Heidegger, 1962). Ironically—given its designation as, at most, a "second-class" constituent of being (see, e.g., Dewey, 1958)—personal experience *is* what makes the scientific pursuit of knowledge about reality possible. Telescopes, microscopes, timing devices, nuclear accelerators, neuroimaging technology, and the host of modern means of obtaining objective knowledge about "reality" are useless absent an experiencing subject. As Gallagher and Zahavi (2008) point out, "Science is performed by somebody; it is a specific theoretical stance towards the world…scientific objectivity is something we strive for but it rests on the observations of individuals" (p. 41). To believe otherwise has the absurd consequence of rendering our knowledge of reality dependent, in its entirety, on the provisions of an experiential conduit stipulated to be nonexistent! At bottom, material reality does not represent so much a discovered fact as a collection of subjectively informed methodological presuppositions, conditioned by metaphysical conceits and justified by the pragmatic serviceability of the products of the scientific enterprise.

With specific regard to the study of human phenomenology, Valera et al. (1993) face the strain between science and the study of mind directly: "When it is cognition or mind that is being examined, the dismissal of experience becomes untenable, even paradoxical. The tension comes to the surface especially in cognitive science because cognitive science stands at the crossroads where the natural sciences and the human sciences meet" (p. 13). They continue:

Neither extreme [*material science or human science*] is workable…. To deny the truth of our own experience in the scientific study of ourselves is not only unsatisfactory; it is to render the scientific study of ourselves without a subject matter. But, to suppose that science cannot contribute to an understanding of our experience may be to abandon, within the modern context, the task of self-understanding. (1993, pp. 13–14, italics added for clarification)

In Chapter 5, I will suggest one way in which a cross fertilization between science and experience might be accomplished.

The Psychological and Physical Aspects of Reality

Harry Potter: "Is this real? Or has this been happening inside my head?"

Professor Albus Dumbledore, the Wizard: "Of course it is happening inside your head, Harry, but why on earth should that mean that it is not real?"

From the movie "Harry Potter and the Deathly Hallows: Part 2" (2011).

Reality, in its most general sense, is often taken to mean everything that has being; that is, everything that exists. Although this conception has been subjected to considerable discussion and emendation over the centuries, current Western science holds there is only one reality, one totality of being—physical reality.

Tulving and Szpunar, in contrast, argue for another reality in addition to the physical—mental reality. Their view is that "Despite doubts that some thinkers, through the ages, have suffered privately or expressed publicly, mental reality is as 'real' as physical reality" (p. 257). In their view, the constituents of mental or psychological reality include such things as sights, sounds, thoughts, love, hate, jealousy, images, memories, ambition, suffering, happiness, beauty, ugliness, dreams, hopes, feelings, beliefs, doubts, wisdom, stupidity, the pull of the past, the anticipation of the future—that is, the processes and states that populate what James (1890) referred to as the "spiritual self" (that is, the part of the self constituted by mental states).

The relationship between physical reality and mental reality, as Tulving and Szpunar (2012) see it, is complicated.

> Although mental reality is utterly dependent on physical reality, in the sense that it could not exist in the absence of physical reality, it also is independent of physical reality in the sense that what exists in mental reality does not exist in physical reality.... There are no thoughts, images, memories...experiences, dreams, feelings, hopes, fears...in physical reality...there is neither personal past nor personal future...there is no self. (p. 258)

They continue, "The converse also is true, there is not a single thing that exists in physical reality that also exists in mental reality. There are no rivers or mountains, trees or flowers, no brain, no blood, no neurons or synapses, no molecules of atoms in mental reality" (Tulving & Szpunar, 2012, p. 258).

While this sounds like Cartesian substance dualism (see, e.g., Descartes, 1984), the authors object to such a categorization.

> Like all other cognitive neuroscientists we accept as axiomatic that mental reality is fully dependent on the brain, is continuous with the brain and the rest of physical reality. The brain and the mind are made of the "same stuff." We do not yet know what that "stuff" is but we have reason to believe that eventually it will be discovered. Contrary to what some people like to declare, we know that the brain and mind are not identical.

> The brain and the mind are different entities constituted of the same basic "stuff." (Tulving & Szpunar, 2012, p. 258).

This position could still be characterized as a form of dualism, albeit a dualism of property rather than of substance.

While I do not necessarily endorse the claim that there *must* be two separate, non-overlapping realities (a single reality, constituted by processes, aspects, and/or entities having non-identical metaphysical commitments, could do the job; e.g., James, 1909/1996, plurality), or embrace the metaphysical assumption that mind and brain necessarily reduce to the same "stuff" (although this view could be accommodated by a version of emergent materialism), I fully agree with Tulving and Szpunar's main conclusion—that phenomena occurring at the level of the mental, though dependent in some way on properties of the physical, are neither reducible to, nor fully explicable in terms of, *purely* materialist considerations. We must, of both practical and theoretical necessity, accord psychological reality its place our inventory of "what is." We would be well advised to deal with experiential offerings at the level at which they manifest in awareness.[7] Fodor (1974) voices this sentiment with characteristic directness, asserting that it is *not* "required that the taxonomies which the special sciences [*e.g., psychology*] employ must themselves reduce to the taxonomy of physics. It is not required, and it is probably not true" (p. 114; italics added for clarification).

In sum, we must remain open to the strong possibility that "reality" is constituted by a plurality of aspects that share different metaphysical commitments. The alternative approach, favored by contemporary science, is to force reality—i.e., "all there is"—into a presently unverifiable materialistic metaphysics. If psychologists adopt the latter approach, we run the risk of stripping away the aspects of human experience that make the experience the experience that it is. If we adopt the former approach, Danziger's (2008) "window" remains open on psychological reality in the richness with which it is given. As Nagel (1974) has argued, personal experience is not something that can be satisfactorily captured via third-party descriptive acts; to be appreciated, experience needs to be experienced (for a related view, see Jackson, 1986).

Chapter 4

The Epistemological
and Ontological Selves:
A Brief "Summing Up"

As I hope now is evident, I draw a sharp conceptual distinction between two types or categories of self, types whose different aspects play a central role in how behavioral scientists should conduct research and theorize about the self. By conflating them, researchers often assume that they are casting light on one (most often the assumed focus of theory and research is the ontological self), while experimentally manipulating the other (the neural-based sources of self-knowledge—the epistemological self).

The distinction between the self as subject and the self as the source of the qualitative features of experience can be summarized as follows.

1. The *ontological self*—the conscious self, experienced as first-person subjectivity (see, e.g., Dainton, 2008; Foster, 1991; Ganeri, 2012; Lund, 2005; Strawson, 2009). Its character as self-awareness means it entails subjectivity, which, in turn, implies that it cannot be treated as an object of analysis (see, e.g., Earle, 1972; Kant, 1998; Klein, 2012a, 2012b; Swinburne, 1997, 2013; von Fraasen, 2005; Zahavi, 1999, 2005). That is, it is not clearly reducible to objectification, measurable neural-cognitive function,

or neurally mediated content, although it is informed (in some manner) and, perhaps, informs (in some manner) the content of experience (Klein, 2012a, 2012b). But the content in awareness (experience) is not to be taken as constituting that awareness (e.g., Kant, 1998). Rather, awareness is the means by which the content is apprehended.

The ontological self is:

1. Occurrent—that is, it is an ever-present (save, perhaps, for episodes of dreamless sleep or vegetative coma) form of experience (see, e.g., James, 1890; Kant, 1998; Lund, 2005; Klein, 2012a; Strawson, 2009);

2. A phenomenological unity—that is, an aspect of self (at least in its synchronic instantiation; see Klein, in press-a; Slors, 2001) given in its fullness—that is, not composed of parts (see, e.g., Dainton & Bayne, 2005; Earle, 1956; Giles, 1997; Kant, 1998; Klein, 2012a, in press-a; Lowe, 2008; Yao, 2005; Zahavi, 2005; for recent discussions of phenomenological unity, see Bayne, 2010; Lowe, 2008);

3. Invariant (which follows from its having no parts or properties to undergo change), despite objects of its awareness being subject to considerable variation (see, e.g., Earle, 1956; Fasching, 2009; Kant, 1998; Klein, 2012a; Klein, in press-a). Thus, while the contents of awareness can and do vary, the experiencing subject remains present and invariant throughout; and

4. Lacking properties, it cannot be directly known (see, e.g., Kant, 1998; Klein, 2012a, in press-a). Rather, it is given as experience and can be sensed only by virtue of its felt presence. While we know about objects by virtue of knowing about their properties, the ontological self is not an object,

and thus our acquaintance comes by virtue of its felt or sensed presence, not via a catalogue of properties.

2. The *epistemological self*—the assumed psycho-physical bases of self experiences. In contrast to the phenomenological and compositional unity of the ontological self, the epistemological self is multifaceted, comprising functionally independent systems of self-knowledge, each of which is propertied by features and processes (primarily neuro-cognitive) of the material body. All mental states have content; that is, they are about something (as Brentano, 1995, puts it, they are "intentional"). The job of the systems of the epistemological self is to provide, in some way or ways, the raw data (as well as highly processed data) for self-experience—that is, they provide the content experienced by the ontological self.

In contrast to the ontological self, the epistemological self differs with respect to invariance: unlike the ontological self, the content of the epistemological self is in constant flux (and is so experienced), although some aspects (e.g., long-term memory, body image) show varying degrees of stability. From a materialist (or emergent materialist; see Bunge, 2010) standpoint, the epistemological self is amenable to scientific study and thus constitutes the major body of empiricism psychologists and neuroscientists refer to when discussing and researching "the self" (see, e.g., Beike, Lampien, & Behrend, 2004; Leary & Tagney, 2012; Neisser & Fivush, 1994; Sedikides & Brewer, 2001; Sedikides & Spencer, 2007; Snodgrass & Thompson, 1997).

An additional word about the epistemological self might be helpful for those struggling to distinguish it from the ontological self. As I use the term, the *epistemological* self is dependent on neural mechanisms that pick out what Kirk's (1974a, 1974b) and Chalmers's (1996) philosophical "zombies" are hypoth-esized to *have* (i.e., behavioral and dispositional states), despite the inability to become aware (i.e., the ontological self) of those states. Specifically, the epistemological self emerges from the neuro-cognitive systems that supply self-knowledge (largely situated in the brain, but interactive with the physical body and its environment), systems that enable the presentation of content apprehended by the ontological self. The content provided by sys-tems mediating the epistemological self concern that subset of information having to do with the person (e.g., one's name, body, personal narratives, personality, personal relationships, physical placement with respect to one's surroundings, feelings, etc.; that is the content James, 1890, held to be part of the "self-as-known"), *not* information about (the vast quantity of) impersonal facts, rules, and conventions known by the person (e.g., 2 + 2 = 4, the sun is hot, dogs are animals, water is wet, cross when the light turns green, etc.).

John Locke argues that "consciousness *alone* makes self" (1689, Bk. II, Ch. 27, Sec. 9, emphasis added). This procla-mation, I suggest, is too extreme. Its extremity results from Locke's failure to fully appreciate that the self consists in a multiplicity of aspects occupying different metaphysical com-mitments (*note*: When Locke uses the word "consciousness," he intends it to mean consciousness. He does not, as is often—incorrectly—believed, mean "memory"; Strawson, 2011b). The co-presence of *both* epistemological self-knowledge and the ontological self-awareness to which it is given is required for our everyday experience of "self." Such ideas, it is worth restat-ing, sit comfortably with Fichte's dictum, "No object without a subject and no subject without an object" (see, e.g., Neuhouser, 1990; though, it must be noted, Eastern wisdom traditions often posit the possibility, in highly trained practitioners of the meditative arts, of consciousness without an intentional object; see, e.g., Forman, 1990). On this view, the conceivability of philosophical "zombies" having a sense of self would, by definition, be permanently foreclosed. Such a discussion, however, is not directly relevant to the subject matter of this book and will therefore not be pursued.

Chapter 5

Empirical Evidence and the Ontological and Epistemological Selves

Considerations of objectification and quantification detailed in Chapter 3 take on particular significance when the phenomena under discussion involve the self—a psychological entity that, as William James (1890) opines, lies at the center of our mental life—the immediate datum around which all else revolves. James minces no words in conveying his feelings about attempting to force self-related experience into a materialist mold: "The worst a psychology can do is so to interpret the nature of [*selves*] as to rob them of their worth" (1890, p. 226, italics added for clarification).

In this section I offer a sustained defense of psychological realism. Thus far, I have drawn a conceptual distinction between the ontological and epistemological selves. However, a conceptual distinction, no matter how well crafted, does not license the conclusion that the distinction holds at the level of personal experience; nor does the fact that scientists have an abstract category for a mental entity guarantee that an ontological correlate exists. A conceptualization that is drawn in an entirely theoretical way is only a discourse about experience, not a rendering of the experience (see, e.g., Valera et al., 1993). What is needed is a means of connecting the theoretical arguments *for*, to the empirical "reality" *of*, the content of experience, in its fullness, as given to the ontological self. In what follows, I attempt to do this by examining evidence provided by the introspective reports of individuals suffering from a very unusual psychological dysfunction—the loss of felt ownership of their mental states.

My approach relies on a person's ability to accurately recount the content of his or her introspections. While introspective techniques suffer from a number of interpretive and methodological problems—for example, the effects of verbalization on the experience verbalized, the completeness of verbal reports, the validity inferences based on analysis of response protocols (for review and discussion, see Ericsson & Simon, 1985; Hurlburt & Schwitzgebel, 2007)—these issues are not insurmountable (see, e.g., Brewer, 1994; Hurlburt, 1990). Accordingly, the use of introspective reports as a primary source of data has enjoyed a considerable resurgence among psychologists during the past several decades (see, e.g., in domains such as autobiographical memories, self, consciousness, temporal projection; see, e.g., Baars, 1988; Conway, Rubin, Spinnler, & Wagenaar, 1992; Fivush & Haden, 2003; Hurlburt, 1993; Klein, 2013a; Mills, 1998; Race, Keane, & Verfaellie, 2011; Nelson, 1989; Rubin, 1986). This is due, in large part, to the unique perspective that introspective data provide on constructs of interest. As Hurlburt and Schwitzgebel (2007) observe, "Even hard-nosed neuroscientists ask their subjects about their subjectively felt experience while in the **fMRI** magnet" (p. 5, bold in original).

My method of investigating the ontological and epistemological selves—a merging of empiricism and phenomenology—attempts to save the phenomena by not saddling the investigator with a false choice between either (a) reducing a phenomenon to numerical values or, having failed to do so, (b) forfeiting a claim to scientific respectability. Rather, my approach to empiricism focuses on the analysis of phenomena at a level that (hopefully) approaches that at which they are given in experience. Specifically, the data I present consist primarily of introspective reports from patients for whom disruptions of the function of ontological and epistemological selves are a part of their occurrent phenomenology.

FUNCTIONAL INDEPENDENCE: INITIAL STUDIES AND THEIR INTERPRETIVE LIMITATIONS

In a previous treatment of the self (Klein, 2012a), I presented several studies in which an individual's systems of the epistemological self-knowledge were partially or fully impaired while the ontological self "appeared" to be intact. The most extreme case was provided by Shewmon, Holmes, and Byrne (1999). They studied four individuals between five and 17 years old who were born with nearly total loss of cerebral cortical function. For such persons, the brain supports life at a subcortical level (e.g., brain stem), but higher mental functions (e.g., those supporting the epistemological self) are absent and thus unavailable to the ontological self.

Under these conditions, the patients, despite lacking the neural machinery necessary for verbal report of subjective experience, behaved in ways consistent with the inference that they possessed intact self-awareness. For example, they oriented toward familiar people and away from unfamiliar, smiled and tracked persons of importance in their lives, discriminated visually (albeit via subcortical visual mechanisms), and responded appropriately to pain and pleasure at both a general and a more specific (e.g., music-appreciation) level. They also discriminated between environments; showed, via facial expressions, preferences and dislikes (for music, people, etc.); had awareness of their own bodies; appeared to enjoy socializing (e.g., being with people, and even were capable of limited interaction); and provided behavioral evidence that clearly indicated to their caretakers whether or not they were conscious.

In short, their behavior did not resemble that of patients for whom the prognosis of permanent vegetative state might meaningfully be applied. The patients showed awareness of both the physical world and their own bodies, and they communicated their awareness via physical acts and facial expressions (see also Owen, Coleman, Boly, Davis, Laureys, & Pickard, 2006). It was *as though* the ontological self, deprived of most, though perhaps not all (remember Fitche's dictum), content from the epistemological self, still struggled to make sense of, and respond to, the situation (internal and external) in which it was positioned.

While such evidence is highly suggestive, it also is highly controversial. Decorticate patients cannot verbally report their subjective experience; accordingly, one must rely heavily on inference to support the argument that patients' subjective sense of self persisted in the absence (or at least severe impairment) of epistemological sources of self-knowledge. While the individuals studied appeared to be conscious, it is indeterminate whether they also were self-conscious. And inferences directed at the mental states of other persons raise a host of justifiable concerns (see, e.g., Wisdom, 1968).

Less extreme cases of disruption (e.g., where the patient's ability to engage in introspective reporting is not at issue) also present interpretive problems. For example, because the ontological self is assumed to be a non-compositional, phenomenological unity (see, e.g., Dainton & Bayne, 2005; Klein 2012a; Lowe, 1996; 2008; Yao, 2005), it has no "parts" to undergo change. In contrast, the epistemological self admits to a multiplicity of features and processes, providing ample opportunity for alteration of its constituents. These presumed differences in composition entail that disruptions of the ontological and epistemological selves must, by definition, be asymmetrical. Partial ablation of neural mechanisms responsible for epistemological self-knowledge in the presence of fully intact personal subjectivity is both permitted and anticipated. Indeed, evidence I have presented (Klein, 2012a) suggests this to be the case. By contrast, the converse—the partial loss of the ontological self in the presence of intact (or largely intact) systems of epistemological self-knowledge—is ruled inadmissible by definition. This is because the ontological self, being a metaphysical simple, is not composed of parts.

In this view, cases that, on the surface, appear to reflect disturbances to self-awareness (for review, see Prignatano & Schacter, 1991) are taken to reflect the intact ontological self struggling to come to terms with the compromised offerings from an impoverished or disordered epistemological self. While a *complete* loss of the ontological self in the presence of intact or partially intact epistemological systems of self-knowledge is consistent with theory, if it occurs, it probably does so only in cases of dreamless sleep and vegetative coma and thus is introspectively unknowable.

Given this built-in asymmetry, inferences about the psychological reality of the ontological and epistemological selves must be based on evidence from demonstrations of *single dissociations* of psychological functions. By the logic of single dissociations, the ontological and epistemological selves are considered two functionally independent systems of self if and only if a variable (e.g., a disease process) differentially affects performance of the latter but not the former.

Consider again, for example, the case of patient D.B. (see, e. g., Klein, Loftus, & Kihlstrom 2002; Klein, Rozendal & Cosmides, 2002). At the time of testing, D.B., a 79-year-old man, had become profoundly amnesic as a result of anoxia following cardiac arrest. As detailed in Chapter 2, he suffered a total dysfunction of the epistemological self's system of episodic memory. These gaping holes in D.B.'s corpus of self-knowledge were met by him with the confusion, concern, and fear one would expect from a coherent, conscious individual not fully able to comprehend the experiential changes wrought by his disease (of which he was only intermittently aware). He was greatly troubled by the absence of information that, as D.B. described it, "I don't know, but I should, shouldn't I?" (D.B. often broke down in tears over his inability to recollect knowledge of his personal past.) In short, information that he expected to inform subjective self-awareness failed to do so.

Thus, for patient D.B., aspects of epistemological self-knowledge were seriously impaired, yet his sense of himself as a singular source of first-person identity appeared to be intact (similar cases from the literatures on amnesia, autism, and dementia are presented in Klein, 2012a). As a result of breakdowns in access to sources of epistemological self-knowledge, the ontological self became increasingly confused and frightened. But, and this is the important point, the ontological self *remained intact* as the center of D.B.'s personal subjectivity. Based on behavioral observations (verbal and physical), individuals suffering epistemological self impairments remain capable of experiencing and voicing the confusion they experience, remain capable of wondering what has happened to them, and, sadly remain capable of fearing their fate (Klein, 2012a, in press-a).[1]

On the surface, cases like D.B.'s appear to offer solid support in favor of the functional independence of the ontological and epistemological selves. Unfortunately, things are not so straightforward. Concerns about the epistemic warrant of inferences derived from cases of single dissociations (see, e.g., Dunn & Kirsner, 1988; Neely, 1989; Teuber, 1955) make it clear that studies such as those I have presented (Klein 2012a) cannot be taken in unequivocal support of the proposition that there are two metaphysically distinct selves. One problem is that finding that a variable (in D.B.'s case, anoxia) had no *observable* effect on his ability to report his subjective experience does not logically entail the conclusion that it had *no* effect on his ontological self. The effect simply may have occurred at an unobservable, and thus unreportable, level. (One might try to counter this concern by noting that it requires the ontological self to be capable of "degrees of function"—an assumption directly contravened by its presumed status as a non-compositional entity. But the assumption of metaphysical simplicity ultimately requires empirical verification; no amount of philosophical analysis or stipulation secures its viability.)

More troubling is the realization that single dissociation *always* can be consistent with a single system model (Dunn & Kirsner, 1988). All that is required is that a single system consist of a variety of mental properties and functions that are differentially susceptible to the influence of internal and external contingencies. Applied to the topic at hand, the demonstration that a function attributed to the epistemological self (e.g., memory) is impaired by a clinical variable (e.g., anoxia) while the ontological self appears to remain unaffected, always can be interpreted as demonstrating that, in actuality, the variable had its effect on a *single* system of self constituted by properties and processes (including self-awareness) that had been (improperly) attributed to two different self systems. Thus, a model in which the assumed properties of the ontological and epistemological selves are folded into a single system of self cannot be ruled out by evidence from single dissociations.

AVOIDING THE PITFALLS OF DISSOCIATIVE ASYMMETRIES: THE ABSENCE OF PERSONAL OWNERSHIP

The demonstration or discovery of a single dissociation thus cannot automatically sanction the conclusion that the self exists as two metaphysically separate aspects of reality. Accordingly, the studies I reported (Klein 2012a), while suggestive, cannot by themselves arbitrate conclusively between a model in which the ontological and epistemological selves represent (a) two separate aspects of reality, or (b) two different ways of thinking about a single aspect of reality—i.e., "the self," taken to consist of the experiences, processes, properties, and causal potencies that, according to a two-self model, populate metaphysically distinct selves.

If a dissociation, whether single or double (since the latter consists of two single dissociations, it inherits many of the interpretive ambiguities that plague the former), does not provide sufficient resolution for distinguishing between a single self or two selves that, while interacting, are separable aspects of reality, then what can be done? In the next section, I present and interpret the results of introspective reports that, I believe, permit a more nuanced and empirically justifiable approach to deciding between single and dual models of self.

The evidence I present and the methods I utilize are not novel. What is novel is identifying the significance of their potential contribution to the issues under consideration. Specifically, I analyze, via introspective reports, a very unusual form of pathology—one in which the direct connection between epistemological and ontological selves becomes severed. This form of disruption results in the loss of personal ownership of the content of experience (i.e., the offerings of the epistemological self) by the subjectivity to which these experiences are given (i.e., the ontological self).

In pathologies of this nature, the content (e.g., a mental state) and perspective ("in my head") both are present to phenomenal awareness, but the sense of personal ownership of content by awareness dissolves. That is, despite maintaining a clear sense of hosting a mental state (i.e., perspectival ownership), the occurrent state no longer is experienced as *belonging* to the ontological self. Its sense of being given to consciousness as "mine" (i.e., its personal ownership) no longer is present. Such experience can be highly confusing and sometimes traumatic. It is found among prefrontal lobotomy patients as well as individuals suffering from clinical syndromes such as depersonalization and schizophrenic thought insertion (for reviews, see Albahari, 2006; Klein & Nichols, 2012; Klein, 2013a; Lane, 2012; Stephen & Graham, 2000).

Disruption of personal ownership provides a fertile ground for testing the theory of two selves. Ownership logically entails a two-part relationship between an owner and the content owned. The demonstration that certain individuals can report personally relevant mental content (i.e., from the epistemological self) in the absence of an experientially given *sense* that this content *belongs* to them (i.e., to the ontological self) would thus go a considerable way toward supporting a claim for the functional independence of these two types of selves. While the content of a mental state still is taken as perspectivally owned (in the sense that it is experienced as inside one's head), it lacks a sense of being personally owned (that is, as owned by the ontological self)—though it can be inferred as belonging despite lacking any direct, pre-reflective feeling of being "mine."

Under these circumstances, both the epistemological and ontological selves maintain their integrity. However, the connection between them is rendered inoperative, resulting in the experience of "hosting," but not personally owning, one's mental states. This, in turn, implies that experience (*contra* James, Kant, and others) is not "stamped" with the quality of "mine-ness"; instead, the relationship between the epistemological and ontological selves is contingent rather than intrinsic (see, e.g., Klein, 2013a; Lane, 2012).[2]

Cases of the Loss of Personal Ownership

Deficits restricted to the loss of personal ownership are not subject to issues that cloud interpretation of single (or double) dissociations. This is because individuals suffering from ownership loss do not suffer from asymmetries in the functional status of the to-be-compared systems; rather, both the epistemological and ontological selves remain intact. Accordingly, questions do not arise concerning issues such as the potential for undetected changes in the "supposedly" unaffected system. What is lost is the "mental glue" that cements the experienced relationship between two separate, unimpaired systems of self as one of belonging. In this manner, the ontological and epistemological selves become uncoupled, thus providing evidence for a functional independence between *what* (content) and *how* (modality) something is experienced and *who* experiences it.

In this chapter I present the evidence from a variety of clinical examples of loss of personal ownership. These studies support the view that the epistemological and ontological selves each merit its own, non-overlapping status as an aspect of reality. I begin with evidence that, while supportive, is not entirely free of controversy. I end with several unusual cases that make the point for functional independence with particular potency.

EVIDENCE FROM FRONTAL LOBOTOMY

Psychosurgery in the form of prefrontal lobotomy consists of the surgical ablation of pathways linking the thalamus with parts of the frontal lobes (see, e.g., Freeman & Watts, 1942). Although no longer practiced—it was conducted primarily from the late 1930s through the early 1970s—its intent was to relieve patients of mental disorders that had proven resistant to all other treatments available. A few days following a "successful" surgical intervention, patients would evidence a lessening of their morbid symptoms (e.g., anxiety, depression), but show no obvious decline in general intelligence or cognitive function. Personality remained largely unchanged. Patients' ability to remember their personal past was mostly unaffected (though patients often remarked that they did not think of their past as often as they had prior to surgery).

One interesting consequence of the procedure was its effect on the postsurgical patients' feeling of self-concern (see, e.g., Robinson & Freeman, 1954). Patients often showed modest or no interest in their future or current circumstances. Some also experienced a form of depersonalization in which the felt boundaries of self had become fuzzy or lost (see, e.g., Freeman & Watts, 1946). Feelings of self-continuity were reduced or eliminated without accompanying loss of the concept (Robinson & Freeman, 1954).

These findings, taken in toto, permit the inference that such individuals maintain largely (though not completely; e.g., the loss of self-continuity) intact epistemological self-knowledge (e.g., personal memories, personality) and apparently unimpaired subjectivity, together with a lack of concern for, or interest in, the self-relevant contents of awareness. This loss of concern, although not identical to loss of ownership, is suggestive.

However, before pursuing a potential analogy between concern and ownership, it is important to point out that the data available are based almost entirely on clinical anecdotes and observations collected for purposes quite removed from questions of personal ownership. Moreover, the absence of concern for the content of self-awareness, while consistent with the idea that patients do not take such content as personally owned, is not mandated by any available data. In short, while findings from patients undergoing prefrontal lobotomy for the relief of psychopathological disorders are suggestive, they do not license strong conclusions about the functional independence of types of selves.

Of greater relevance to questions of personal ownership is one particular aspect of the psychosurgical process—the finding that surgery can alter patients' reactions to pain without changing their ability to experience pain. That is, patients experienced no loss of the sensation of pain following lobotomy, only relief from mental suffering.

As a result of this finding, psychosurgery subsequently was adopted as a medical intervention for dealing with chronic organic pain (see, e.g., *JAMA*, 1950; Freeman & Watts, 1946, 1948). Since this procedure often was conducted on individuals lacking attendant psychopathology (e.g., schizophrenia)—which might compromise the ability to pinpoint whether behavior suggesting an apparent lack of personal ownership was due to (a) the surgical separation of the frontal lobes from other neural structures, or (b) pre-existing clinical conditions, such as delusional states, that might compromise the interpretation of self-reports—the data it provides are more amenable to answering questions concerning a connection between self-content (i.e., pain) and the personal ownership of that content. Specifically, the results of psychosurgery for pain are consistent with the view that, postoperatively, the patients simultaneously experienced pain while distancing themselves from the experience. This, in turn, is consistent with the possibility that what is taking place in these individuals is not the absence of experienced content or the lack of awareness of that content, but rather a failure to connect the content to the self (i.e., the absence of personal attachment or concern for an experientially given mental event).[3]

Although instructive, studies of the effects of psychosurgery on pain were not designed with the purpose of testing a functional independence between types of selves. Accordingly, one must exercise considerable caution drawing inferences from the data. While it seems reasonable to see in such data some form of disruption between self-relevant content and personal subjectivity (as manifested by the absence of concern), the data require a considerable number of assumptions before such conclusions can emerge.

Pain Asymbolia

An additional question about lobotomy patients is whether they *fail* to react to pain or whether their apparent indifference stems from a *reduced* reaction to pain. For example, there are reports that in some cases lobotomized patients, despite professing a lack of concern about experienced pain, still withdraw from situations associated with serious pain (e.g., avoiding walking on a broken leg; e.g., Melzack & Wall, 1985). Thus despite their professed indifference, they appear to react to strong pain in a manner one would expect someone experiencing pain to react. Of course, behavioral reactions to situations associated with the induction of pain are not unambiguously informative about the nature of the pain experience (e.g., Long, 1965). Nonetheless, here is an additional problem making sense of the data obtained from lobotomized patients.

More promising are reports of patients suffering pain asymbolia—a rare condition associated with lesions in the insula cortex (specifically, the posterior insula), in which patients report that they feel a pain, recognize it as pain, but show no tendency to remove themselves from the cause of the pain (e.g., (e.g., Grahek, 2007). In short, such patients show both phenomenological *and* behavioral indifference to pain. Interestingly, reports suggest that they also show little, if any, interest in avoiding situations they know are likely to result in pain (e.g., Hemphill & Stengel, 1940).

As Colin Klein (2011) notes, individuals suffering pain asymbolia often appear indifferent (both motorically and emotionally) to the experience of pain as well as its potential relevance to bodily self-preservation. Pain occurs, but patients no longer appear to care: They are unmoved by the experience of pain and act as though they see no need to reduce or remove themselves from situations causing, or likely to cause, pain. This combination—intact experience of pain and intact understanding of the meaning of that experience conjoined with an absence of concern for its personal relevance—fits nicely with the idea that what these patients lack is *not* the experience of pain (the ontological self) or knowledge that pain is occurring within one's body (the epistemological self), but rather the ability treat the content of experience as "mine" (i.e., personally owned).

Unfortunately, as C. Klein (2011) also notes, such patients show clear similarities to the syndrome known as depersonalization. They thus suffer the interpretive ambiguities surrounding that disorder (to be discussed in the section titled "Depersonalisation"—see below). However, it is important to at least consider the possibility that pain asymbolia constitutes an instance of a loss of personal (certainly not perspectival) ownership, and thus may have important implications for the functional independence of the ontological and epistemological self.

EVIDENCE FROM PSYCHOPATHOLOGY

Thought Insertion

The idea that the experience of ownership of one's mental states can come loose from those states is not a novel observation. A substantial literature (primarily clinical) speaks to its reality. Particularly relevant is the phenomenon of "thought insertion," often occurring in schizophrenic patients manifesting delusional symptoms. Patients experiencing thought insertion report that there is a thought in their minds that they did not themselves voluntarily produce. That is, they do not see their thoughts "first-personally" as their own; they do feel they are the *authors* of their own mental states (see, e.g., Bortolotti & Broome, 2009; Frith, 1992; Gallagher, 2000; Northoff, 2000; for review, see Fernandez, 2010; Stephen & Graham, 2000).

Unfortunately, the experiences of schizophrenic patients clearly are delusional. A delusion, roughly speaking, is a belief maintained without due sensitivity to the evidence for or against it, and without appropriate regard for the causes of the belief or for the consequences of holding it. This leaves reports of those suffering from thought insertion open to the objection that the experiences reported are tainted, to some indeterminate degree, by aspects of psychopathology having little, if anything, directly to do with their experience of selves, per se. Accordingly, such data, though on the surface consistent with the argument for the reality of separate selves, cannot, by themselves, provide closure.

Anosognosia

There are patients suffering from a variety of problems with memory, language, perception, or voluntary movement who appear to have no awareness of their deficits. This lack of awareness of a mental deficit was named *anosognosia* by Babinski (1918; for review, see McGlynn & Schacter, 1989; Prigatano & Schacter, 1991). Anosognosic patients may acknowledge some difficulty in their impaired domains, but they attribute their problems to something besides their own deficits. It should be understood that these patients' behavior is not mere denial of a deficit or indifference to it (when a patient acknowledges a deficit but seems unconcerned about it, the syndrome is called *anosodiaphoria*).

Anosognosia is a real danger to the patient, of course. People who do not realize that they are paralyzed on one side are headed for disaster if they should try to get up; those who do not realize they are blind on one side are unlikely to take special steps to avoid obstacles and oncoming objects on the affected side. In the dementing disorders, such as Alzheimer's disease and even schizophrenia, anosognosia is particularly insidious because it occurs in the late stages of illness (see, e.g., McGlynn & Kaszniak, 1991; Mograbi, Brown, & Morris, 2009), when the patient is most impaired.

From an ownership perspective, one wants to know what these patients make of their own behavior, given that they do not acknowledge their deficits. Some patients attribute their inability to move to arthritis or rheumatism rather than paralysis; others, when asked to move the affected limb, appear distracted or move the unaffected limb or respond that they have moved the affected limb, when in fact they have not (this even happens when patients look at the affected limb during the examination).

Patients' explanations can sometimes become bizarre or delusional. For example, a patient may claim that the affected limb is not his or her own, but rather belongs to someone other than the self—e.g., forgotten by a previous patient, or belonging to someone else lying at their side (often doing something naughty). One woman studied by Bisiach and Geminiani (1991) was anosognosic for her hemiplegia. She claimed that her left hand did not belong to her, but rather had been forgotten in the ambulance by another patient. She acknowledged that her left shoulder was her own and agreed with the inference that her left arm and left elbow also were her own, because they were attached to her left shoulder, but this inference did not extend to her left hand (she could not explain why that hand carried her wedding ring). Another hemiplegic patient stated that his left arm belonged to the examiner. When the examiner placed the patient's left hand between his own two hands, the patient continued to deny that his arm and hand were his own and attributed three arms and three hands to the examiner!

Viewed from the lens of "loss of personal ownership", many (though not all) cases of anosognosia suggest relatively uncompromised epistemological self-knowledge (e.g., an intact ability to present visual images of all but the affected body parts to the ontological self in an uncompromised manner) existing alongside an intact ontological self (e.g., the ability to recognize these contents in awareness). What has come undone is primarily (but not necessarily exclusively—see below) the link that enables the content to be given directly and pre-reflectively to the ontological self as "mine": the person acknowledges the visual presence of an "afflicted" limb, but fails to experience that presence as personally owned. Interestingly, in some of the cases mentioned, the patient seemed unable to utilize inferential procedures to compensate for the loss of a sense of ownership (e.g., the patient who felt the examiner must possess three hands).

Anosognosia represents a diverse collection of afflictions, varying considerably both in the bodily function compromised and the extent to which the patient is able to acknowledge the presence of dysfunction. It also typically occurs in cases of psychopathology (e.g., dementia, schizophrenia) and/or neural insult. While the latter (neural damage) is not necessarily troubling from an interpretive standpoint (it is to be expected that neural damage underlies loss of experienced bodily ownership—though the nature of the damage may compromise interpretation of the focal pathology—i.e., ownership loss), the former (comorbidity) suggests that, while informative, cases of anosognosia are delusional and thus present interpretive difficulties similar to those raised in regard to thought insertion. In addition, the status of the epistemological self's body image often is compromised to some degree by the disorder (see, e.g., Prigatano & Schacter, 1991), making it difficult to ascertain the extent to which the designation of "intact," applied to the epistemological self, is truly an accurate representation of its clinical status.

Depersonalization

A less contentious domain in which to seek evidence for the independence of the ontological and epistemological selves via loss of personal ownership is the psychiatric syndrome known as *depersonalization* (for reviews, see, Guralnik, Schmeidler, & Simeon, 2000; Hunter, Phillips, Chalder, Sierra, & David, 2003; Reustens, Nielson & Sachdev, 2010; Sierra & Berrios, 1997; Simeon, 2004; Simeon & Abugel, 2006). Depersonalization, which can be either transient or chronic, is characterized by a sense of detachment from one's sense of self (see, e.g., Medford, Sierra, Baker, & David, 2005). As defined by *The Diagnostic and Statistical Manual* (DSM-IV-TR), depersonalization is an alteration in the perception or experience of the self so that one feels detached from, and as if one is an outside observer of, one's mental processes or body (American Psychiatric Association, 2004). It affects approximately 1% to 2% of the general population (primarily in its transient form) and perhaps as much as 23% of the psychiatric population (Simeon, 2004).

Individuals suffering from depersonalization describe the experience as feeling separate from oneself, feeling disconnected from or outside of one's thoughts and emotions, separated from one's own being, feeling empty and incomplete, feeling of a lack of appropriation or attribution of mental states to the self (see, e.g., Sierra & Barrios, 1997; Simeon, 2004; Simeon & Abugel, 2006). Interestingly, functional neuroimaging has identified abnormal

activity in the prefrontal regions in patients experiencing depersonalization (see, e.g., Phillips et al., 2001; reviewed in Medford
et al., 2005), which, taken in conjunction with the findings from
prefrontal lobotomy, suggests that neural substrates in the frontal cortex may play a role in the experience of loss of personal
ownership.

Patients experiencing depersonalization thus show a persistent
or recurrent sense of being detached from their mind and bodies,
a lack of personal ownership of the psycho-physical "me," a feeling
that one's body and mental states do not belong to the self. In such
instances, it appears that a fully functioning psycho-physical self
exists in conjunction with a fully functioning self of first-person
subjectivity, albeit a subjectivity bewildered by the absence of felt
ownership of the content of its experiences. As Albahari (2006,
pp. 173–174) observes, depersonalized patients "realize there is
something wrong and they *wish the state and its attendant sensation would go away*...the negative emotions arise because the person is in a situation he wishes was otherwise" (italics in original).
Depersonalized patients thus appear to evidence an intact epistemological and ontological self conjoined with the loss of a direct
sense of a personal relationship between the two.

However, chronic depersonalization (the far more prevalent
form) is found primarily in individuals suffering from comor-
bidities such as depression, schizophrenia, anxiety disorders, and
panic attacks (see, e.g., Medford et al., 2005; Reutens et al., 2010).
Research also has shown extensive comorbidity (in approximately
60% of patients) with Axis II personality disorders, including
borderline, avoidant personality, and obsessive-compulsive personalities (see, e.g., Simeon, 2004). In light of these attendant
psychopathologies, the testimony of individuals suffering from
depersonalization inherits many of the concerns afflicting cases

of thought insertion and anosognosia regarding the "purity" of introspective reports, thus calling into question the utility of such evidence for clear insight into the nature of selves.[4]

EVIDENCE FROM NON-PSYCHOPATHOLOGICAL CASES OF LOSS OF PERSONAL OWNERSHIP

Although patients afflicted with anosognosia, depersonalization, and thought insertion all evidence an apparent loss of personal ownership of their thoughts, issues of comorbidity render their introspective reports less than optimal for our purposes. There are, however, a very few cases reported in the literature in which the loss of one's sense of personal ownership of one's thoughts takes place in the absence of any apparent psychopathology. These "pure" cases provide a clearer window into the possibility of a separation between the epistemological and ontological selves.

While such cases constitute an extremely small database (I know of only two "pure" cases), I suspect additional cases will begin to appear with greater frequency once dysfunction of content-ownership becomes a more widely recognized pathology (see also Lane, 2012). Once assembled, such cases will permit investigators to empirically document and formally test the effects of "loss of ownership" on self experience. I discuss two such cases next.

Loss of Perceptual Ownership

Zahn et al. (2008) report the case of D.P., a 23-year-old male who complained of "double vision." After examination, it was established that D.P. did not actually experience double vision; rather, he was able to see everything normally, but "he did not immediately recognize that he was the one who perceives and that he needed a second step to become aware that he himself was the one who perceives the object" (p. 398). This "second step" entailed the use of inference—to circumvent the absence of experientially given personal ownership of the content of awareness—to establish, by virtue of its location (i.e., in his head), that a perceptual experience was his own.

Although diagnosed with right inferior temporal hypometabolism, dysfunction of the right parieto-occipital junction and precentral cortex, in *all* other respects—e.g., psychiatric, neuropsychological, cognitive, medical—D.P. appeared perfectly healthy. He suffered from no apparent psychosocial stressors or trauma and was socially well integrated. Administration of a structured DSM-IV-TR interview did not result in any psychiatric diagnosis. Additional testing revealed normal memory performance, visual object recognition, lexical retrieval, attention and executive function. Importantly, his visual perceptions were unaccompanied by delusions, thought insertion, obsessive doubts, compulsions, or fear. In short, other than a highly circumscribed experienced loss of ownership of his visual perceptions, and the distress it engendered, D.P. seemed perfectly normal.

D.P.'s pattern of spared and preserved function is consistent with the proposition that his epistemological self is fully functional, as is his ability to become aware of the contents of that self, with one critical exception: While the content of his visual perceptions coexists with ontological self-awareness (i.e., he is aware of and perplexed by the fact that perceptual content are not experienced as personally owned), the former no longer is experientially given to the latter *as* personally owned. Accordingly, the case of

D.P. offers strong support for the idea that the epistemological and ontological selves demonstrate functional independence under circumstances in which concerns about the epistemological warrant of his introspective reports are not colored by concerns about comorbidity.

Loss of Memory Ownership

Another study—for which far more extensive introspective reports are available—is the case of patient R.B. (The details of this case are summarized herein. For fuller treatment, see Klein & Nichols, 2012.) As a result of a being hit by a car while riding his bicycle, R.B. suffered severe physical injuries, including a crushed pelvis and the fracturing of almost all of the ribs on the left side of his torso. In addition to these physical traumas, he suffered several transient cognitive impairments, including mild aphasia and both retrograde and anterograde amnesia for events in close temporal proximity to his accident. Performance on tests of verbal fluency and short-term memory span fell slightly below scores provided by neurologically healthy, age-matched controls. R.B.'s psychological profile, in contrast, presented a clinical healthy and socially well-adjusted individual.

To alleviate the pain he endured, R.B. initially was placed on a morphine drip, followed by pain medication administered orally. As the intensity of his pain subsided, he weaned himself off medication. Importantly, at the time of being tested for experienced personal ownership, R.B. was not on any pain medication. In addition, his memory impairments, aphasia, and verbal fluency deficits had resolved.

However, not all cognitive function returned to normal. Specifically, R.B. could intentionally recall specific events temporally and spatially situated in his personal past (i.e., what I have labeled "the episodic offerings of the epistemological self," System #1), but those memories were compromised in a very unusual manner: The retrieved events were unaccompanied by a sense of personal ownership. That is, R.B. was able to remember pre-injury incidents from his life, accompanied by clear temporal, spatial, and self-referential content. But he did not *feel* that the content he experienced belonged to him. In his own words, they lacked a sense of "personal ownership" (in the descriptive language of William James, 1890, his memories lacked feelings of "warmth and intimacy"). Absent a feeling of ownership, his ability to experience those memories as emanating from his personal past was lost. R.B.'s memory ownership issues lasted approximately three months.

This type of memory impairment—intact content of recollection absent a sense of personal ownership—has not, to my knowledge, previously been documented in the amnesic literature (Klein, 2013a; Klein & Nichols, 2012).[5] As an example of this form of impairment, following his release from the hospital, R.B. provided a description of what it was like for him to recall personal events:

I did not own any memories that came before my injury. I knew things that came before my injury. In fact, it seemed that my memory was just fine for things that happened going back years in the past [the period close to the injury was more disrupted]. I could answer any question about where I lived at different times in my life, who my friends were, where I went to school, activities I enjoyed. But none of it was "me." It was the same sort of knowledge I might have about how my parents met or the history of the Civil War or something like that.

Again:

> I could clearly recall a scene of me at the beach in New London with my family as a child. But the feeling was that the scene was not my memory…the memories did not in any way feel like they were my memories.

Although it might appear that R.B.'s reports are semantic memory–based personal facts (i.e., System #3 of the epistemological self) rather than episodic recollections, extensive documentation and analysis make it clear this is *not* the case (as R.B. clearly observes, "I am remembering scenes, not facts").[6] The content of his introspective accounts (Klein & Nichols, 2012) clearly adheres to the criteria for episodic memory—i.e., that the memories provide a person with a record of the temporal, spatial, and self-referential features of the context in which original learning took place (see, e.g., Dere, Easton, Nadel, & Huston, 2008; Tulving, 1972, 1983, 1985, 1995; for recent review, and suggested emendations, see Klein, 2013a). By these criteria, R.B.'s descriptions of his memorial experience leave no doubt about the episodic nature of his recollective content—i.e., it is appropriately situated in time and space, not factual, atemporal, semantic knowledge (e.g., Tulving, 1983). Moreover, R.B. clearly is the subject of his recollections. But these recollected contents are presented to awareness absent a sense of being personally owned. That is, despite his memory content's including perceptual evidence that he is the subject of his memorial experience, felt ownership of his recollections has to be *inferred* rather than *directly given* to the ontological self.

R.B. can thus acknowledge the inherent "pastness" of an occurrent mental event. To do so, however, inferential processes must be carried out on the content of his experience. His pre-reflective, non-inferential sense that the memory is part of his ontological self is no longer coincident with his awareness of the memory experience. This perplexing circumstance—which can be taken as an instance of what philosophers refer to as *quasi-memory* (see, e.g., Klein & Nichols, 2012; Shoemaker, 1970; Slors, 2001)—is made clear by R.B. in the following observation:

> I can picture the scene perfectly clearly…studying with my friends in our study lounge. I can "relive" it in the sense of re-running the experience of being there. But it has the feeling of imagining, (as if) re-running an experience that my parents described from their college days. It does not feel like it was something that really had been a part of my life. Intellectually I suppose I never doubted that it was a part of my life. Perhaps because there was such continuity of memories that fit a pattern that lead up to the present time. But that in itself did not help change the feeling of ownership.[7]

He continues:

> Having been to MIT had two different issues…my memories of having been at MIT I did not own. Those scenes of being at MIT were vivid, but they were not mine. But I owned "the fact that I had a degree from MIT"…that might have simply been a matter of rational acceptance of fact.…I remember eating pizza at XXX in Isla Vista, but the memory belongs to someone else. But knowing I like pizza, in the present, now, is owned

by me. When I recall memories from my past, I intellectually know they are about me. It just does not feel like it.

Thus, R.B. vividly remembers where a specific event transpired, when a specific event took place, and that it involved him. However, the memorial offerings of his epistemological self are not directly given to the ontological self as "mine." Rather, that connection must be forged via inferential procedures. While R.B. can infer that the events recalled *must* be of past personal experiences, he does not know this by virtue of a *direct feeling* of "mine-ness" present in awareness (for further discussion, see Klein, 2013a).

This peculiar disconnection also is reflected in the way R.B. treats his pre-injury memory content—both during the loss of experienced "givenness" as well as following its eventual "reunion" with the ontological self (at which point, epistemological self-content previously experienced as "unowned" regained its sense of personal belonging):

When I did "take ownership" of a memory, it was actually quite isolated. A single memory I might own, yet another memory connected to it I would not own. It was a startling experience to have no rhyme or reason to which memories I slowly took ownership of, one at a time at random over a period of weeks and months.

He continues:

What happened over the coming months...was interesting. Every once in a while, I would suddenly think about something in my past and I would "own" it. That was indeed something "I" had done and experienced. Over time, one by one, I would come to "own" different memories. Eventually, after perhaps eight months or so, it seemed as if it was all owned...as if once enough individual memories were owned, it was all owned. For example, the MIT memory, the one in the lounge...I now own it. It's clearly part of my life, my past.

Other systems of R.B.'s epistemological self (e.g., personality traits, semantic facts about the self, personal identity, self-continuity) appeared, at least within the limits of testing, largely unaffected by ownership issues:

> SBK: Can you recall who you are? More specifically, what you were like and what you are like—that is, your trait characteristics. If so, are your traits felt as your own?
>
> RB: Yes, I know what I am like...intelligent, shy, honest, a good person, things like that? Yes, I definitely have no identity problem. And the memories created since the injury I have full ownership of. Things that are in the present, like my name, I continue to own.

An interest in and an ability to plan one's future is a core criterion for inferring the presence of experienced self-continuity (see, e.g., Klein, in press-a). In this regard, R.B. (unlike many lobotomy patients) shows no obvious impairment. Describing the challenges he faced when attempting to formulate personal plans, R.B. reports:

> During the un-owned period I was able to plan for the future. Although my working memory loss and lack of skill at compensation made it challenging...the best compensation I found was to separate the planning of the strategy from the execution.

It worked best if I made a list of "Things to Do." Then I could
handle doing them one at a time.

In short, R.B. maintains a robust sense of personal identity
and self-continuity (for discussion, see Klein & Nichols, 2012). He
has unimpaired, conscious access to his semantic self-knowledge
(both trait and factual) and episodic personal narratives (Klein,
2013a). This content, substantiated by third-party sources, and
its availability to awareness, strongly suggest that both the epistemological and ontological selves are intact in patient R.B. His
problem centers exclusively on his disrupted experience of "content ownership."

SUMMING UP

Examination of individuals suffering from a condition in which
the content presented to awareness becomes divorced from the
feeling that it is personally owned provides solid support for the
existence of two individually intact, independent selves. While
the cases presented vary in clarity of resolution—ranging from
reports potentially tainted by concomitant psychopathologies
(e.g., thought insertion, anosognosia, depersonalization) to the
descriptions of relatively well-circumscribed deficits of ownership
unfettered by issues of comorbidity (e.g., D.P., R.B.)[8] —the data
they provide, taken as a whole, point strongly to the functional
independence of the epistemological and ontological selves.

Equally important, the connection between the two selves
does not appear to be intrinsic. Rather, it is one of contingency
(Klein, 2013a). When the sense of personal ownership—which

serves as the bridge spanning the metaphysical gap between the two selves—is rendered dysfunctional, the connection between selves is not totally lost; however, it transitions from being directly given, to being one in which the relationship is based on logical inference. This inference appears to be performed *by* systems of the material brain *on* content supplied by the epistemological self—content that, once determined (via considerations such as semantic self-knowledge and "in-the-head" perspective) to be factually self-relevant (as opposed to pre-reflectively given), is taken as an aspect of self by first-person subjectivity. This process of inference is, in effect, the "second step" used by patient D.P. (Zahn et al., 2008) to gain an appreciation that he was the one who perceived an object present in his awareness.

One issue that needs to be addressed concerns the "type or degree" of independence between selves warranted by the data presented. While the evidence argues for a functional independence, it does not provide direct support either for or against the metaphysical separation of the ontological and epistemological selves. And, since there are abundant examples (see Chapter 2) of functional independence between systems of self-knowledge *within* the epistemological self, could we not argue that in non-clinical cases there is a *single* self, but that this self can get fragmented in pathological conditions? Put differently, the epistemological and ontological self might represent two systems within a single self, systems that under normal circumstances work together in a particular way. In certain pathologies they do not work together in "that way," and this produces a peculiar kind of first-personal experience. The epistemological systems of self-knowledge are still available to the systems producing self-awareness, since content provided by the epistemological self still is "in the head" of those suffering pathologies of personal ownership. What is missing is recognition of the unity, and this makes the afflicted individual's first-person experience unusual.

The upshot, one could argue, is not that there are two metaphysically separate types of selves, but that there is one self that, under certain conditions of clinical dysfunction, has certain problems of self-recognition. A thought experiment proposed by philosopher John Perry may help clarify this interpretation. Imagine a person walking through a store looking at a trail of sugar and wondering about the careless person with a leaking bag of sugar in his cart—until he realizes that he is that person. The fact that he could think about "the person with the leaking sugar bag" and not know that it was he does not mean that he is not that person, only that he does not see himself as such.

In response, I admit that I find no basis on which to claim that the empirical data provide more than advertised—i.e., evidence for the functional independence of two aspects of self. Other considerations, however, can be marshaled (and have been; see Chapter 3) in support of a metaphysical separation as well. Specifically, the logical distinction between the "subject having an experience" and the "object of that experience" supports the claim of a metaphysical difference between the epistemological and ontological selves. Also, concerns about the possibility of a material as well as an immaterial self are exactly what motivate most of the objections raised about causal interaction across metaphysical levels. To assume that the material (i.e., epistemological self) and immaterial (i.e., ontological self) aspects of reality might be folded into a single self-system would add a considerable burden to the metaphysical work required of the term "single."

Taken in isolation, nothing in the empirical data supports more than functional independence. And that is all it was intended to do. The argument for a metaphysical difference trades on additional philosophical analysis and metaphysical arguments. If the reader feels more comfortable with the idea that the epistemological and ontological selves are different features of one self, albeit features having considerably different metaphysical facets, nothing of great importance is lost regarding the main argument that the self consists of two aspects of reality that have very different metaphysical commitments.

This clearly is a very difficult issue, one that cannot (in any obvious manner) be resolved by experimental demonstration. William James struggled with this as well. While in his early work on the self (see, e.g., James, 1890) he often regarded the self as a single entity composed of various parts and functions, his later work reveals his ongoing concern with the idea that the self can be taken as a unity; rather he felt the need to seriously entertain the idea that different aspects of reality contributed to the human experience of self (cf. James, 1909/1996).

In short, any speculation concerning the metaphysical status of hypothesized aspects of reality needs to be treated with great caution. What is not in doubt is that questions about the functional independence (absent any strong metaphysical commitments) of the epistemological and ontological selves appear amenable to empirical analysis. Introspective reports from a variety of patients converge on this conclusion, and, in the process, provide empirical justification for the proposal that the self of apparent material instantiation and the self of apparent conscious awareness represent two functionally independent aspects of what we call the self.[9]

Chapter 6

Some Final Thoughts

My stance is this: Ultimately, we will not make progress coming to terms with our object of inquiry—the self—until we acknowledge that the self is a *multiplicity*, consisting of (at least) two intimately related, yet metaphysically separable, aspects of the term "self" (i.e., the ontological and epistemological selves). Until we not only recognize, but fully embrace the different "types" or "aspects" of selves we routinely conjoin in both our thought and research, progress on what Chalmers (1996) has described as the "hard problem" is likely to remain elusive.

In this book, I have attempted to ground this conceptual distinction between types of selves with empirical analysis. While such a project is commonplace when dealing with material aspects of reality, it is subject to critique when used to examine aspects assumed to occupy different metaphysical levels of being. In particular, the ontological self, defined as (potentially immaterial) self-awareness, falls victim to well-known limitations of adopting a scientific analysis to explore non-quantifiable aspects of reality (see, e.g., Baars, 1988; Valera et al., 1993; Wallace, 2003). The demonstration that, at least in certain cases of "loss of personal ownership," each self remains fully (or largely) functional, but that the relationship between them is compromised, provides initial support (of an empirical flavor) for the contention that the epistemological and ontological selves enjoy existence as functionally independent aspects of reality.

It is of importance that my discussion of types of selves is empirical as well as theoretical. There is no doubt that both selves can be known on the basis of reflection on one's personal experience. They are "selves of acquaintance," in Bertrand Russell's (1912/1999) sense. In addition, the epistemological self also is amenable to knowledge by description. Both aspects of self merit the attention of anyone who claims he or she relies on empirical methods, broadly construed. However, in traditional science, such phenomena (particularly the partition of selves into ontological and empirical) often remain hidden from view due to the normally seamless and flawless way in which they are interwoven. Another impediment to their discovery is that most scientists still are reluctant to engage in the direct study of first person experience (their own and that of others; e.g., Hurlburt & Schwitzgebel, 2007; Wallace, 2003).

Hopefully, that is changing. Scientists are becoming more flexible (for example, there is an increasing willingness to consider data obtained from introspective reports as empirical evidence) and willing to carry out the necessary experiments (particularly as regards investigations into consciousness). As Ricard and Thuan (2001) observe,

> If we define the terrain field of science as what can be physically studied, measured, and calculated, then right from the start we leave out everything that is experienced in the first person, and all immaterial phenomena. If we forget this limitation, then we soon start affirming that the universe is everything that can be objectified in the third person, and only what is material. (p. 241).

Some of the strategies necessary for a conceptual reorientation of our metaphysical commitments are already available (as discussed and employed in this book). Their under-utilization largely reflects the failure of scientists to ask the "right" questions (Lane, 2012). As this gradually changes—and I strongly believe that it will—aspects of reality will unfold in ways unimaginable within the shackles of a purely materialist metaphysics.

I have argued that the ontological self is a subjective unity (see, e.g., Antoneitti et al., 2008; Lowe, 2008; Strawson, 2009; White, 1990). While it can apprehend diverse aspects of reality—both mental and physical—those acts of observation simply serve to bring a diverse world of external and internal content to the apprehension of the subject. And since that subject is, of necessity, one, the diverse aspects in its subjective field necessarily are unified.

Our subjective unity is the result of the unity of the observing subject. As Earle (1955) notes, "Unity presides over every act of the mind, it is subjective, and it is in principle distinguishable from any real objective unity" (p. 54). He continues, "I am not any of the things I apprehend, and yet they all stand in my presence, and appear to me. The I to which all things can appear is the ultimate problem. It seems to be both nothing and yet relatable to everything" (p. 55). Perhaps the problem ultimately will be clarified. As of now, the mystery remains.

Possibly we need a new, more inclusive, metaphysics (see, e.g., Earle, 1955; Feyerabend, 1979; Fodor, 1974; Gendlin, 1962; Kitchener, 1988; Martin, 2008; Meixner, 2008; Papa-Grimaldi, 1998; Valera et al., 1993), one in which reality is not reduced to *only* that which can be manipulated by current scientific methods. Reality is too broad to be captured by a single approach. Nor do we currently have any way of surveying the whole of reality. To maintain that *all* reality can be captured by a *single* set of methods (e.g., scientific) is to maintain that reality consists in its entirety of objects, processes, systems, and relationships; i.e., only of those aspects capable of being grasped by a particular set of methodologies and theoretical assumptions. Quoting Earle again (1955, p. 89),

> We have no way of surveying the whole of reality; we have only a formal idea of it on one hand, and an infinitesimally small assortment of unclear objects on the other...we must in other words hold our theory in precisely that tension which represents our honest position; we *don't* know what the entire character of reality is, and we should not attempt to close our ignorance through impatience with the infinity of the absolute itself.

Meixner (2008) voices similar concerns, focusing his critique directly on the materialist dogma of modern science:

> Materialism is regarded as being identical with, or implied, by, the scientific worldview. But it is never inquired whether there even is such a thing as the *scientific worldview*....Indeed, are there not more worldviews than one that are not only compatible with, but actually *good for* science? Perhaps there even is a worldview that is better for science than the materialistic one? (p. 157; emphases in original)[1]

A similar perspective, but more directly relevant to the issue at hand (i.e., the ontological and epistemological selves as objects of study), is offered by Gendlin, who calls for

> add[ing] a body of theory consisting of concepts of a different type—concepts that can refer to experiencing, and that can

grasp the way in which experience functions [to] ... distinguish this different order of concepts from logical and objective concepts, and to provide systematic methods for moving back and forth between the two orders. (Gendlin (1962, p. 7)

Pointing directly at the heart of the matter, clinician and theoretician Carl Rodgers asks, "Is there some view...which might preserve the values of...scientific advances...and yet find more room for the existing subjective person who is at the heart and base even of our system of science?" (cited in Gendlin, 1962, p. 48). The point is that the scientific methods that currently dominate psychology do not (and perhaps cannot) directly tap the heart of our discipline—subjectivity.

It is unreasonable to try to fill in our ignorance of the scope of reality with theories that describe only the pieces of the whole that can be apprehended by our sense organs (with or without external aid) and our reason—i.e., the objective, material world. As noted philosopher C. B. Martin (2008) concluded, after devoting himself to a study of these issues for more than half a century, if we wish to understand reality—its properties and the causal interactions manifested therein—"New and basic ways of thinking are needed" (p. 197). To posit that the ontological self is capable of being grasped by such finite aspects of reality as matter, energy, or, more abstractly, universal laws, processes, or Platonic forms, is a very restrictive enterprise—one that presupposes we have warrant to declare (without concrete evidence) that reality, in its fullness, can be captured by such constructs (e.g., Feyerabend, 1979; Gendlin, 1962; Jackson, 1986; James, 1909/1996; Margenau, 1984; Papa-Grimaldi, 1998; Valera et al., 1993; van Fraasen, 2005).

I do not reject a scientific approach to reality. Science has proven an immensely successful way to question nature and has greatly enhanced our understanding of the aspects of reality it is designed to deal with (indeed, my career has been informed by and devoted to it). What I do take issue with is the assumption (typically implicit) that the scientific method has exhausted our ways of apprehending and knowing reality. Render to science what belongs to science, but we should not surrender all of reality too hastily, lest we fail to appreciate great mysteries that are not accommodated by its particular set of assumptions and methodologies.

There have increasingly been calls for attempts to unify our knowledge of reality (see, e.g., Damasio, et al., 2001), but many of these attempts have been predicated on the belief (again, typically implicit) that the scientific approach should serve as the foundation from which unity springs (e.g., Kosso, 2007). We do not need, nor do I believe it possible, to embrace the world, in its fullness, via an enterprise wherein unity is little more than a code-word for scientific reduction (e.g., Earle, 1955; Hyman, 2007; Koestler & Smythies, 1967; Papa-Grimaldi, 1998; Vaihinger, 1925).

The views of self I have articulated—the self of science and the self of experience—both are real, both are valid; but it is important not to conflate them, to reduce the sensed self of conscious awareness to the neuro-cognitive self of empirical exploration. An all-too-common refrain is that science is not science unless it involves the quantitative treatment of material reality. With regard to quantification, many great advances have been made by expressing reality in terms of mathematically formulated physical laws (see, e.g., Nagel, 2012; Rescher, 1996; Spencer Brown, 1957). Measurements and equations are supposed to sharpen thinking. But, as often as not, they tend to make the thinking non-causal and fuzzy. They become the objects of scientific manipulation instead of auxiliary tests of crucial inferences. Many—perhaps most—of the great issues of facing psychology are qualitative, not quantitative. Equations and measurements can be useful when they are related to experience; but experience comes first. With regard to materialism, it is undeniable that many, if not all, of the great achievements in modern science were made possible by the exclusion of "mind" from the world around us. However, as Nagel (2012) has argued, at some point "it will be necessary to make a new start on a more comprehensive understanding [*of reality*] that includes the mind" (p. 8; italics mine).

What we need is a unity of knowledge that considers *all* aspects of experience as real (in this sense, my approach is far less dualistic than it might, to some, appear), and attempts to understand those experiences using *all* the tools currently available, with particular emphasis on the most complex tool of all—the human mind.

Our goal should be to establish a common ground between a neuro-cognitive science and human experience. Only in this way can our appreciation for, and understanding of, our ability to experience ourselves as thinking, feeling, wanting, and doing beings— experiences that probably are what gave rise to psychology in the first place (Humphrey, 1984)—be constructively engaged.

On a more speculative note (I appreciate that the reader may feel that the phrase "more speculative" in the present context is a logical impossibility!), I see "mental ownership" as the "glue" that unites two metaphysically distinct aspects of reality—the material and the non-material. Ownership is a means by which the interdependence of the whole is achieved—that is, it breaks down metaphysical duality by enabling a non-dualistic, intimate, reflexive union between the self of material instantiation and the self of conscious awareness.

NOTES

Preface

1. Rescher (1984) also is concerned with the question of whether all truths contained within a formal system (e.g., scientific) can be proved from within that system. He concludes that explanatory (though not descriptive) completeness *is* a realistic goal for science. To circumvent the Godelian consequence that explanatory completeness is unattainable due to an unending iteration of meta-formalizations, Rescher adopts a pragmatic solution: "In the final analysis…we explain the system-as-a-whole through its capacity to 'do the job' (i.e., functional sufficiency) of scientific rationalization." (1984, p. 13, parentheses added). Substituting pragmatic criteria for analytic argument, however, comes at the cost: By stipulating a purely pragmatic resolution, the logical force of Godel's incompleteness theorem remains fully intact (though curtailed via a somewhat arbitrary and vague criterion—i.e., how much "of the job" is required to "do the job"?).

Chapter 1

1. In this chapter I focus on ideas of the self from the perspective of Western intellectual traditions. The issues addressed also have received considerable attention from Eastern philosophy. Readers interested in the overlap between the ideas expressed herein and those of Eastern thought are referred to Chadha (2013) and Ganeri and Klein (in preparation).

2. The decision to place Hume in the company of theorists marking the self as an illusion is based on his famous "bundle theory of introspection" (Hume, 1739–1740/1978). However, as is well known, Hume struggled mightily with his views on the self (see, e.g., Baxter, 2008; Biro, 1976; Schwerin, 2012; Strawson, 2011). Given his concerns about bundle theory (appearing in the Appendix to his *Treatise of Human Nature*), it is open to discussion whether Hume deserves to be included with theorists who view the self as merely a flight of the imagination.

3. Strawson (2009) points out an additional concern about the type of knowledge about the self we can derive based on its function as a prefix. Consider, for example, the prefix "self" in "self-experience" and "self-regulating." In the former case, "self" is used to identify a certain qualitative type of experience (i.e., that had by the self). The function of "self" in "self-comparison," in contrast, is similar to the function of "self" in terms such as "self-sealing" or "self-adhesive": "Self-comparison" does not necessarily imply the comparative functions of a self, any more than being "self-adhesive" implies the adhesive properties of the self. The function of "self" in such two-part relations primarily is reflexive, having no obvious conceptual implications for the self, per se.

4. It is worth mentioning here that, although my proposed distinction between types of selves has a clear affinity to James's (1890) distinction between self-as-knower and self-as-known, his self-dichotomy does not, strictly speaking, imply a distinction between entities. Rather, he speaks of the different functions, or levels, of a common entity—the self—conceptually joined by the notion of reflexivity. In short, James's self-as-knower and the self-as-known represent two different ways of thinking about one aspect of self, rather than two metaphysically separate, but related, aspects. As we will see, however, his metaphysical stance changed over the years, and by the early 1900s he was questioning whether reality might best be conceived as a plurality of aspects (James, 1909/1996).

5. Hume famously had a problem with the self: "When I enter most intimately into what I call myself I always stumble on some particular perception or other...I never catch myself at any time without a perception and never can observe anything but the perception" (1739–1740/1978, p. 252). His issue with self, often termed Hume's "bundle theory" of perception, is that, on introspection, he can identify the content of his experience, but has no recognition of an experiencer. Thus, he worries, "where is the self?" As noted in note 2, Hume's inability to find the self (as captured in bundle theory) troubled him considerably, leading him to emend his ideas in the Appendix to his *Treatise*. However, per the view proposed in this book, he need not have been so vexed. What he observed introspectively were the objects of experience (e.g., perceptions), not the subject having the experience. Nor could he

observe the latter. As we will see, Hume's perplexing experience is exactly what we would expect on the basis of the distinction I propose between the epistemological self (the neural-cognitive systems that supply the content of experience) and the ontological self (the self of first-person subjectivity). As will be argued (extensively) in this book, the former can be treated as an object of experience and thus is fully (or partially, depending on conditions) introspectable. The latter, being subject, rather than object, is not introspectable—it is sensed, rather than known or thematized—and thus cannot be an object of one's perception (e.g., Earle, 1972; Husserl, 1964; Klein, 2012a; Zahavi, 2005).

Thus, Hume's failure to find his own subjectivity is not a reasonable objection to its existence. In point of fact, he was looking for the wrong thing in the wrong way. His metaphysical or methodological presuppositions prevented him (or anyone engaging in a similar enterprise) from recognizing that the ontological self is not something one can find by inner reflection.

6. This treatment of episodic and semantic memory follows closely the view adopted by most contemporary psychologists. However, in a recent paper I have challenged certain aspects of the received view, arguing, for example, that what makes a memory episodic or semantic is not the memory content per se, but the manner in which that content is presented to awareness (Klein, 2013a). This is not the place to discuss the merits of my definitional emendations. However, the reader should be aware that, like so much in science, our concepts are not static—rather, they evolve to accommodate new findings and theoretical developments.

Chapter 2

1. I have not included the environment (social, cultural, and physical) and its reciprocal influence on the person. I fully appreciate their obvious relevance for what it means to have knowledge of one's self. For example, what I am calling the *epistemological self* (and the autobiographical memory component in particular; see, e.g., Bruner, 2002; Eakin, 2008; McAdams, 1993; Nelson, 2003) is substantially socio-cultural in both its nature and expression (for review, see Fivush & Haden, 2003; see also the Symbolic Interactionist positions of Mead, Cooley, and many others; as well as James, 1890, on the *social* self).

However, I have chosen to localize my claims about the constituents of the epistemological self at the level of neural architecture. Accordingly, social, cultural, and situational self-knowledge is folded into—and thus contained within—the neural machinery provided by systems of memory. This may be a vast oversimplification (as, indeed, is suggested by consideration of mirror neurons, Theory of Mind processes, and other neural structures that appear unique to social cognition rather than cognition taken more generally; see Klein, 2013c). I acknowledge that my selection criteria may be overly restrictive, but considerations of textual flow suggest that an explicit, and possibly lengthy, discussion of social/cultural considerations would be more diverting than beneficial.

Chapter 3

1. For classic, sustained defense of the composite view of self/consciousness, see Brentano (1995) and Hume (1739–1740/1978). However, I believe what Hume and Brentano had in mind with their talk of "bundles" and "separable" versus "distinctional parts" are the phenomenal content of the pre-reflective (Zahavi, 2005) or ontological (Klein, 2012a) self, not the self taken as the venue within which content is given to awareness.

2. It is worth mentioning that many of the proposed properties of the epistemological and ontological self fit reasonably well with what Kant appears to have had in mind when he contrasts the non-entitive status of the transcendental self (the thinking subject that I am) with empirical sources of self-relevant cognition. For Kant, "I" is always a subject and never a predicate. The self cannot be grasped as an object, and is abiding or constant in a temporal sense. What undergoes change are the presentations of content to the cognizing self. As Kant observes, "For in that which we call the soul, everything is in continual flux, and it has nothing abiding except perhaps (if one insists) the I, which is simple only because this representation has no content [*i.e., it is not an object*]" (1998, p. 432; italics mine). The self, for Kant, is only the consciousness of my thinking; while we have direct experience that a subject exists, we know nothing about what that subject is.

   One must, however, exercise caution when discussing Kant's views on the self, as his usage varies across treatments. The I in *Refutation of Idealism* refers to that aspect of the self that can be introspected—the empirical ego; the I in the *Transcendental Deduction* refers to the subjectivity performing the introspection (these distinctions map nicely on the epistemological and ontological selves of the present discussion).

3. This "given-ness" (as I hope to show in the penultimate chapter of this book) can, however, come undone (see, e.g., Gott, Hughes, & Whipple, 1984; Klein & Nichols, 2012; Vallar & Ronchi, 2009; Zahn, Talazko, & Ebert, 2007), revealing the epistemological and ontological selves to be functionally independent aspects of reality.

4. In a carefully reasoned critique of many of the criteria for existence—such as principles of individuation, separation, causal closure, energy conservation, spatio-temporal continuity—Hoffman and Rosenkrantz (1994) conclude

that material substances are no better off than immaterial entities with respect to these criteria. Many of the standard philosophical objections to the existence of immaterial being thus cannot be depended on to demonstrate that immateriality is unintelligible.

5. Unfortunately, as the principle of inductive pessimism (Stanford, 2006) makes clear, today's certainties probably will be tomorrow's misconceptions. As Poincaré (1952) notes, "Every age has scoffed at its predecessor, accusing it of having generalized too boldly and too naïvely." (pp. 140–141). Thus, our scientific ideas concerning how things work, at any present moment, may well prove untenable (e.g., Kuhn, 1962; Rescher, 2000).

6. Readers might be interested in whether things change if super strings are substituted for subatomic particles (i.e., the quark family of the standard model) as the assumed fundamental building blocks of reality. They do not. According to string theory, the dimensions of a sting are approximately 10^{-33} cm, situating it comfortably in the region of quantum indeterminacy. Thus, whether one adopts quarks or strings as one's fundamental constituent of reality, the argument holds—reality cannot be described by contemporary physics, and it eludes any conceptual framework we are currently capable of devising.

7. Indeed, to decree that all of reality comprises exclusively material entities and their interactions is not only to render incomprehensible the means of *knowing* reality, but also to reduce the term "psychological reality" to an oxymoron.

Chapter 5

1. In Klein (2012a) I offered a number of examples of the functional independence of the epistemological and ontological selves. The examples largely were interpretations of the experiential reports from patients suffering unusual neuro-cognitive impairments (e.g., complete episodic amnesia, chronic depersonalization).

   One does not have to search the archives of neurological oddities to find evidence of dissociation between selves. An example likely to resonate with the reader's personal experience involves the act of awakening from a deep (and presumably dreamless) sleep. Proust nicely captures the phenomenology in his monumental work *Remembrance of Things Past* (1981). The book's narrator, on awakening, observes:

   "…I awoke in the middle of the night, not knowing where I was. I could not even be sure at first who I was: I only had the most rudimentary sense of existence … but then the memory … would come like a rope let down from the heavens and draw me out of the abyss of not-being from which I could never have escaped by myself" (p. 5).

Proust's description is particularly telling with regard to the argument for the functional independence of selves. On awakening, the narrator is conscious but lacks content with which to anchor his awareness. He has only "a rudimentary sense of existence". In my terms, the narrator's ontological self is present, but it has yet to reestablish its psycho-physical bearings. The situation resolves quickly when memory "like a rope let down from the heavens" (the "rope" can be taken as a metaphor for re-forging the connection between ontological self-awareness and epistemological self-knowledge) enables him to experience a unified sense of self.

2. Fuller treatments of "loss of personal ownership" can be found in works by Albahari (2006), Fasching (2009), Klein (2013), Klein and Nichols (2012), Lane (2012), and Synofzik, Vosgerau, and Newen (2008).

3. Some may wonder whether hypnotic treatment of chronic pain warrants a similar interpretation. It does not. In the standard treatment of pain by hypnosis, what is changed is the intensity of experience of pain, rather than personal attachment to that experience (see, e.g., Jensen & Patterson, 2006).

4. Another form of psychopathology that might appear relevant to questions about the self seen through the lens of "experienced ownership of one's thoughts" is the Capgras syndrome. Persons suffering from Capgras syndrome experience the delusion that a friend, spouse, parent, or other close family member has been replaced by an identical-looking imposter (for reviews, see Bourget & Whitehurst, 2004; Edelstyn & Oyebode, 1999; Hirstein & Ramachandran, 1997; Sinkman, 2008). However, Capgras typically occurs in conjunction with schizophrenia and dementia (see, e.g., Forstl, Almeida, Burns & Howard, 1001; Silvia & Leong, 1992), rendering it susceptible to many of the same interpretive concerns raised about depersonalization and thought insertion. In addition, the phenomenology of individuals so afflicted is not a sense of alienation from the content of their mind, but rather a form of derealization—i.e., the feeling that people, objects, or surroundings are unreal or artificial (see Reutens et al., 2010). It thus bears more on the meaning of one's perceptions than it does on ownership of one's perceptually driven mental states.

5. There is, however, evidence that one of the symptoms accompanying depersonalization is the feeling that one had not been involved in one's personal memories (Sierra, Baker, Medford, & David, 2005).

6. A thorough analysis of R.B.'s memories makes it clear that they fit the traditional criteria for episodic recollections rather than memory of semantic facts. The interested reader is referred to Klein and Nichols (2012) and Klein (2013a).

7. All of R.B.'s memories were substantiated by third parties as valid renditions of events that actually transpired in his life.

8. R.B.'s inability to recognize himself as the owner of his memories is not a delusion but a cognitive impairment, a fact that is manifested in his determined

and eventually successful efforts to reclaim those memories as his own. It is hard to understand what it could mean to claim that the episodic memories of a normal, healthy (save for his ownership impairment) person are all delusions, let alone to claim this precisely because they involve the loss of personal ownership. At best there is a "delusion" in the same sense in which one might say that the senses "delude" us into thinking we see continuous movement when in fact what we see are sequences of frames, and other innocuous ways in which brain processes deceive conscious awareness. This, though, is to use the term "delusion" to mean any strange, false belief, rather than a belief held in spite of the evidence and without regard to its harmful consequences (whether true or false).

9. The case of R.B. also suggests that the sense of numerical personal identity is quite narrowly circumscribed: R.B. had factual self-knowledge, trait self-knowledge, and knowledge of personally experienced episodes, but he did not have a pre-reflectively given sense of continuity with his past person. His apparent deficit was in representing, from the first person, "I had these experiences." That is, his impairment entailed a loss of the ability to directly connect personally experienced content with ontological self-awareness.

Chapter 6

1. A reasonable question is, "Why, given the concerns raised in this book, has materialism become the pre-eminent metaphysical stance of Western science and philosophy?" One reason is simply that it is the correct position to take. But, as I hope I have shown, while this might be the case, there is no formal or empirical support for such a conclusion. Meixner (2008) addresses this question from the perspective of the sociology of science, showing that factors having little to do with scientific principles or logical analysis play a major role in the pre-eminence accorded materialism.

REFERENCES

Aczel, A. D. (2001). *Entanglement: The greatest mystery in physics.* New York: Four Walls Eight Windows Press.

Afriat, A., & Selleri, F. (1999). *The Einstein, Podolsky and Rosen paradox.* London: Plenum Press.

Ahern, C. A., Wood, F. B., & McBrien, C. M. (1998). Preserved vocabulary and reading acquisition in an amnesic child. In K. Pribram (Ed.), *Brain and values* (pp. 277–298). Mahwah, NJ: Erlbaum.

Albahari, M. (2006). *Analytical Buddhism: The two-tiered illusion of self.* Houndsmills, UK: Palgrave Macmillan.

Almog, J. (2002). *What am I? Descartes and the mind-body problem.* Oxford, UK: Oxford University Press.

American Psychiatric Association. (2004). *Diagnostic and statistical manual of mental disorders, text revision (DSM-IV-TR).* Washington, DC: R.R. Donnelley & Sons.

Antonietti, A. (2008). Must psychologists be dualists? In A. Antonietti, A. Corradini, & E. J. Lowe (Eds.), *Psycho-physical dualism: An interdisciplinary approach* (pp. 37–67). Boulder, CO: Rowman & Littlefield Publishers, Inc.

Antonietti, A., Corradini, A., & Lowe, E. J. (2008). *Psycho-physical dualism: An interdisciplinary approach.* Boulder, CO: Rowman & Littlefield Publishers, Inc.

Arcaya, J. M. (1989). Memory and temporality: A phenomenological alternative. *Philosophical Psychology, 2,* 101–110.

Baars, B. J. (1988). *A cognitive theory of consciousness.* New York: Cambridge university Press.

Babinski, J. (1914). Contribution a l'etude des troubles mentaux dans l'hemiplegie organique cerebrale (anosognosie) [Contribution to the study of mental disturbance in organic cerebral hemiplegia (anosognosia)]. *Revue Neurologie,* *1,* 845–848.

Babinski, J. (1918). Anosognosie [Anosognosia]. *Revue Neurologie, 31,* 365–367.

Baillie, J. (1993). *Problems in personal identity.* New York: Paragon House.

Baker, M. C., & Goetz, S. (2011). *The soul hypothesis.* New York: The Continuum Internations Publishing Group. Babinski, J. (1918). Anosognosie [Anosognosia].

Balaguer, M. (2010). *Free will as an open scientific problem.* Cambridge, MA: The MIT Press.

Baron-Cohen, S. (1995). *Mindblindness: An essay on autism and theory of mind.* Cambridge, MA: MIT Press.

Baron-Cohen, S., Leslie, A. M., & Frith, U. (1985). Does the autistic child have a "theory of mind"? *Cognition, 21,* 37–46.

Bartlett, F. C. (1932). *Remembering.* London: Cambridge University Press.

Batthyany, A., & Elitzur, A. (2006). *Mind and its place in the world: Non-reductionist approaches to the ontology of consciousness.* Frankfurt, Germany: Ontos Verlag.

Baxter, D. L. M. (2008). *Hume's difficulty.* London: Routledge.

Bayne, T. (2010). *The unity of consciousness.* Oxford, UK: Oxford University Press.

Beck, F. (2008). Mind, brain, and dualism in modern physics. In A. Antonietti, A. Corradini, & E. J. Lowe (Eds.), *Psycho-physical dualism: An interdisciplinary approach* (pp. 69–97). Boulder, CO: Rowman & Littlefield Publishers, Inc.

Beck, F., & Eccles, J. C. (1992). Quantum aspects of brain activity and the role of consciousness. *Proceedings of the National Academy of Sciences, 89,* 11357–11361.

Beike, D. R., Lampinen, J. M., & Behrend, D. A. (2004). *The self and memory.* Hove, UK: Psychology Press.

Bell, J. S. (1993). *Speakable and unspeakable in quantum mechanics.* New York: Cambridge University Press.

Bennett, M. R., & Hacker, P. M. S. (2003). *Philosophical foundations of neuroscience.* Malden. MA: Blackwell Publishing, Ltd.

Berkeley, G. (1710/2003). *A treatise concerning the principles of human knowledge.* Mineola, NY: Dover Publications, Inc.

Bickle, J. (2003). *Philosophy and neuroscience: A ruthlessly reductive account.* Boston, MA: Kluwer Academic Publishers.

Biro, J. I. (1976). Hume on self-identity and memory. *The Review of Metaphysics, 30,* 19–38.

Bisiach, E., & Geminiani, G. (1991). Anosognosia related to hemiplegia and hemianopia. In G. P. Prigatano & D. L. Schacter (Eds.), *Awareness of deficit after brain injury: Clinical and theoretical issues* (pp. 17–39). New York: Oxford University Press.

Bohm, D. (1980). *Wholeness and the implicate order*. London: Routledge & Kegan Paul.

Bohr, N. (1934). *Atomic theory and the description of nature*. Cambridge, UK: Cambridge University Press.

Bohr, N. (1958). *Atomic physics and human knowledge*. New York: John Wiley & Sons.

Bortolotti, L., & Broome, M. (2009). A role for ownership and authorship in the analysis of thought insertion. *Phenomenology and the Cognitive Sciences, 8*, 205–224.

Boucher, J., & Bowler, D. (2008). *Memory and autism*. Cambridge, UK: Cambridge University Press.

Bourget, D., & Whitehurst, L. (2004). Capgras syndrome: A review of the neurophysiological correlates and presenting clinical features in cases involving physical violence. *Canadian Journal of Psychiatry, 49*, 719–725.

Bower, G. H. (1972). Perceptual groups as coding units in immediate memory. *Psychonomic Science, 27*, 217–219.

Bower, G. H., & Gilligan, S. G. (1979). Remembering information related to one's self. *Journal of Research in Personality, 13*, 420–432.

Brentano, F. (1995). *Descriptive psychology*. London: Routledge.

Brewer, W. F. (1994). Autobiographical memory and survey research. In N. Schwarz & S. Sudman (Eds.), *Autobiographical memory and the validity of retrospective reports*. (pp. 11–20). New York: Springer-Verlag.

Brown, N. R. (1993). Response times, retrieval strategies, and the investigation of autobiographical memory. In T. K. Srull & R. S Wyer (Eds.), *Advances in social cognition* (Vol. 5; pp. 61–68). Hillsdale, NJ: Erlbaum.

Bruner, J. (2002). *Making stories: Law, literature, life*. New York: Farrar, Straus & Giroux.

Bunge, M. A. (2010). *Matter and mind: A philosophical inquiry*. New York: Springer.

Buss, D. M., & Craik, K. H. (1983). The act frequency approach to personality. *Psychological Review, 90*, 105–126.

Caddell, L. S., & Clare, L. (2010). The impact of dementia on self and identity: A systematic review. *Clinical Psychology Review, 30*, 113–126.

Calkins, M. W. (1915). The self in scientific psychology. *Psychological Bulletin, 12*, 495–524.

Caramazza, A., & Shelton, J. (1998). Domain-specific knowledge systems in the brain: The animate inanimate distinction. *Journal of Cognitive Neuroscience, 10*, 1–34.

Casey, E. S. (1979). Perceiving and remembering. *The Review of Metaphysics, 32*, 407–436.

Cassam, Q. (1994). *Self-knowledge*. Oxford, UK: Oxford university Press.

Cermak, L. S. (1984). *The episodic-semantic memory distinction in amnesia*. In. L. R.

Squire, & N. Butters (Eds.), *Neuropsychology of memory* (pp. 45-54). New York: Guilford Press.

Chadha, M. (2013). The self in early Nyaya: A minimal conclusion. *Asian Philosophy, 23*, 24–42.

Chalmers, D. J. (1996). *The conscious mind: In search of a fundamental theory.* New York: Oxford University Press.

Chisholm, R. M. (1969). On the observability of the self". *Philosophy and Phenomenological Research, 30*, 7–21.

Churchland, P. S. (1986). *Neurophilosophy: Toward a unified science of the mind-brain.* Cambridge, MA: MIT Press.

Clare, L., Whitaker, C. J., Nelis, S. M., Martyr, A., Markova, I. S., Roth, I., Woods, R. T., & Morris, R. G. (in press). Self-concept in early stage dementia: Profile, course, correlates, predictors and implications for quality of life. *International Journal of Geriatric Psychiatry.*

Collins, R. (2008). Modern physics and the energy-conservation objection to mind-body dualism. *American Philosophical Quarterly, 45*, 31–42.

Conway, M. A. (2005). Memory and the self. *Journal of Memory and Language, 53*, 594–628.

Conway, M. A., Rubin, D. C., Spinnler, H., & Wagenaar, W. A. (1992). *Theoretical perspectives on autobiographical memory.* London: Kluwer Academic Publishers.

Cosmides, L., & Tooby, J. (2000). Consider the source: The evolution of adaptations for decoupling and metarepresentation. In D. Sperber (Ed.), *Metarepresentations: A multidisciplinary perspective* (pp. 53–115). New York: Oxford University Press.

Crovitz, H. F., & Schiffman, H. (1974). Frequency of episodic memories as a function of their age. *Bulletin of the Psychonomic Society, 4(5B)*, 517–518.

Dainton, B. (2008). *The phenomenal self.* New York: Oxford University Press.

Dainton, B., & Bayne, T. (2005). Consciousness as a guide to personal persistence. *Australian Journal of Philosophy, 83*, 459–571.

Dalla Barba, G. (2002). *Memory, consciousness and temporality.* Norwell, MA: Kluwer Academic Publishers.

Damasio, A. R. (1994). *Descartes error: Emotion, reason, and the human brain.* New York: G. P. Putnam's Sons.

Damasio, A. R. (1999). *The feeling of what happens: Body and emotion in the making of consciousness.* Orlando, FL: Harcourt, Inc.

Damasio, A. R., Harrington, A., Kagan, J., McEwen, B. S., Moss, H., & Shaikh, R. (Eds.) (2001). *Unity of knowledge: The convergence of natural and human science* (Vol. 935). *Annals of the New York Academy of Sciences.* New York: NY.

Danziger K. (2008). *Marking the mind: A history of memory.* Cambridge, UK: Cambridge University Press.

Dennett, D. C. (1991). *Consciousness explained.* Boston, MA: Little, Brown and Company.

Dere, E., Easton, A. Nadel, L. & Huston, J.P. (2008). *Handbook of episodic memory*. Amsterdam, The Netherlands: Elsivier.

Descartes, R. (1984). *The philosophical writings of Descartes, 2 volumes*. Cambridge, UK: Cambridge University Press (edited by J. Cottingham).

Dewey, J. (1958). *Experience and nature*. New York: Dover publications, Inc.

Dunn, J. C., & Kirsner, K. (1988). Discovering functionally independent mental processes: The principle of reversed association. *Psychological Review, 95*, 91–101.

Duval, C., Desgranges, B., de la Sayette, V., Belliard, S., Eustache, F., & Piolino, P. (2012). What happens to personal identity when semantic knowledge degrades? A study of the self and autobiographical memory in semantic dementia. *Neuropsychologia, 50*, 254–265.

Eakin, P. J. (2008). *Living autobiographically: How we create identity in narrative*. Ithaca, NY: Cornell University Press.

Earle, W. (1955). *Objectivity: An essay on phenomenological ontology*. New York: The Noonday Press.

Earle, W. (1956). *Memory. The Review of Metaphysics, 10*, 3-27.

Earle, W. E. (1972). *The autobiographical consciousness*. Chicago, IL: Quadrangle Books.

Ebbinghaus, H. (1885/1913). *Memory: A contribution to experimental psychology*. New York: Teacher's College, Columbia University. (Translated by H. A. Ruger & C. Bussenius).

Eccles, J. C. (1994). *How the self controls its brain*. New York: Springer-Verlag.

Eddington, A. (1929). *Science and the unseen world*. New York: Macmillan.

Eddington, A. (1958). *The philosophy of physical science*. Ann Arbor, MI: The University of Michigan Press.

Edelman, G. M. (1989). *The remembered present*. New York: Basic Books, Inc.

Edelstyn, N. M. J., & Oyebode, F. (1999). A review of the phenomenology and cognitive neuropsychological origins of Caprgras syndrome. *International Journal of Geriatric Psychiatry, 14*, 48–59.

Einstein, A. Podolsky, B., & Rosen N. (1935). Can quantum-mechanical description of physical reality be considered complete? *Physical Review, 47*, 777–780.

Elvee, R. Q. (1992). *The end of science? Attack and defense: Nobel conference XXV*. Lanham, MD: University Press of America, Inc.

Emmet, D. (1985). *The effectiveness of causes*. Albany, NY: State University of New York Press.

Ericsson, K. A., & Simon, H. A. (1985). *Protocol analysis: Verbal reports as data*. Cambridge, MA: The MIT Press.

Fasching, W. (2009). The mineness of experience. *Continental Philosophical Review, 42*, 131–148.

Feinberg, T. E. (2009). *From axons to identity: Neurological explorations of the nature*. New York: W. W. Norton & Company.

Feinberg, T. E., & Keenan, J. P. (2005). *The lost self: Pathologies of the brain and identity*. New York: Oxford University Press.

Frenandez, J. (2010). Thought insertion and self-knowledge. *Mind & Language*, 25, 66–88.

Fields, C. (2012). If physics is an information science, what is an observer? *Information*, 3, 92–123.

Feyerabend, P. (1979). *Against method: Outline of anarchistic theory of knowledge.* New York: Verso.

Fivush, R., & Haden, C. A. (Eds.) (2003). *Autobiographical memory and the construction of a narrative self: Developmental and cultural perspectives.* Mahwah, NJ.: Lawrence Erlbaum Publishers.

Flanagan, O. (2002). *The problem of the soul.* New York: Basic Books.

Fodor, J. A. (1974). Special sciences (Or: The disunity of science as a working hypothesis). *Synthese*, 28, 97–115.

Forman, R. K. C. (1990). *The problem of pure consciousness.* Oxford, UK: Oxford University Press.

Forstl, H., Almeida, O. P., Burns, A. M., & Howard, R. (1991). Psychiatric, neurological and medical aspects of misidentification syndrome: A review of 260 cases. *Psychological Medicine*, 21, 905–910.

Foster, J. (1991). *The immaterial self.* New York: Routledge.

Freeman, W., & Watts, J. W. (1942). *Psychosurgery.* Springfield, IL: Charles C. Thomas.

Freeman, W., & Watts, J. W. (1946, June 29). Pain of organic disease relieved by prefrontal lobotomy. *The Lancet*, 953–955.

Freeman, W., & Watts, J. W. (1948). Psychosurgery for pain. *Southern Medical Journal*, 41, 1045–1049.

Frith, C. D. (1992). *The cognitive neuropsychology of schizophrenia.* East Sussex, England: Erlbaum/Taylor & Francis.

Gallagher, S. (2000). Philosophical conceptions of the self: Implications for cognitive science. *Trends in Cognitive Sciences*, 4, 14–21.

Gallagher, S. and Cole, J. (1995). Body schema and body image in a deafferented subject. *Journal of Mind and Behavior*, 16, 369–390.

Gallagher, S., & Shear, J. (1999). *Models of the self.* Thorverton, UK: Imprint Academic.

Gallagher, S., & Zahavi, D. (2008). *The phenomenological mind.* New York, NY. Routledge.

Galton, F. (1879). Psychometric experiments. *Brain*, 2, 149–162.

Ganeri, J. (2012). *The self: Naturalism, consciousness, and the first-person stance.* Oxford, UK: Oxford University Press.

Ganeri, J., & Klein, S. B. (in preparation). *Temporal subjectivity: The self and Indian theories of memory and mind.*

Ganellen, R. J., & Carver, C. S. (1985). Why does self-reference promote incidental encoding? *Journal of Experimental Social Psychology*, 21, 284–300.

Gendlin, E. (1962). *Experiencing and the creation of meaning: A philosophical and psychological approach to the subjective.* Evanston, IL: Northwestern University Press.

Gergen, K. J. (1971). *The concept of self.* New York: Holt, Rinehart, & Winston, Inc.

Gertler, B. (2011). *Self-knowledge.* New York: Routledge.

Giles, J. (1997). *No self to be found.* Lanham, MD: University Press of America.

Gillihan, S. J., & Farah, M. J. (2005). Is self special? A critical review of evidence from experimental psychology and cognitive neuroscience. *Psychological Bulletin, 131,* 76–97.

Gott, P. S., Hughes, E. C., & Whipple, K. (1984). Voluntary control of two lateralized conscious states: Validation by electrical and behavioral studies. Neuropsychologia, *22,* 65–72.

Graheck, N. (2007). *Feeling pain and being in pain.* Cambridge, MA: MIT Press.

Green, J. B., & Palmer, S. L. (2005). *In search of the soul: Four views on the mind-body problem.* Downers Grove, IL: InterVarsity Press.

Greenberger, D., Reiter, L., & Zeilinger, A. (1999). *Epistemological and experimental perspectives on quantum mechanics.* Boston, MA: Kluwer Academic Publishing.

Greenwald, A. G. (1975). Consequences of prejudice against the null hypothesis. *Psychological Bulletin, 82,* 1–20.

Greenwald, A. G. (1981). Self and memory. In G. H. Bower (Eds.), *The psychology of learning and motivation* (Vol. 15; pp. 201–236). New York: Academic Press.

Guralnik, O., Schmeidler, J., & Simeon, D. (2000). Feeling unreal: Cognitive processes in depersonalization. *American Journal of Psychiatry, 157,* 103–109.

Guth, A. (1981). Inflationary universe: A possible solution to the horizon and flatness problems. *Physical Review, D23,* 347–356.

Guth, A. (1997). *The inflationary universe.* New York: Addison-Wesley.

Hamerhoff, S. R., & Penrose, R. (1996). Conscious events as orchestrated space-time selections. *Journal of Consciousness Studies, 3,* 36–53.

Hanson, N. R. (1958). *Patterns of discovery: An inquiry into the conceptual foundations of science.* Cambridge, UK: Cambridge University Press.

Hanson, N. R. (1971). *Observation and explanation.* San Francisco, CA: Harper & Row, Publishers.

Hasker, W. (1999). *The emergent self.* Ithaca, NY: Cornell University Press.

Hehman, J., German, T. P., & Klein, S. B. (2005). Impaired self-recognition from recent photographs in a case of late-stage Alzheimer's disease. *Social Cognition, 23,* 116–121.

Heidegger, M. (1962). *Being and time.* New York: Harper & Row, Publishers.

Heisenberg, W. (1958/1999). *Physics and philosophy.* Amherst, NY: Prometheus Books.

Hemphill, R, & Stengel, E. (1940). *A study of pure word-deafness. Journal of Neurology and Psychiatry, 3*, 251–262.

Hetherington, S. (2007). *Self-knowledge*. Plymouth, UK: Broadview Press.

Hirstein, W., & Ramachandran, V. S. (1997). Capgras syndrome: A novel probe for understanding the neural representation of the identity and familiarity of persons. *Proceedings of the Royal Society, London, B., 264*, 437–444.

Hoffman, J., & Rosenkrantz, G. S. (1994). *Substance among other categories*. Cambridge, UK: Cambridge University Press.

Hood, B. (2012). *The self illusion: How the social brain creates identity*. New York: Oxford University Press.

Horst, S. (2007). *Beyond reduction: Philosophy of mind and post-reduction philosophy of science*. New York: Oxford University Press.

Hume, D. (1739–1740/1978). *A treatise of human nature*. Oxford, UK: Oxford University Press.

Hume, D. (1748/2004). *An enquiry concerning human understanding*. New York: Dover Publications.

Humphrey, N. (1984). *Consciousness regained: Chapters in the development of mind*. New York: Oxford University Press.

Hunter, E. C. M., Phillips, M. L., Chalder, T., Sierra, M., & David, A. S. (2003). Depersonalisation disorder: A cognitive-behavioral conceptualization. *Behavior Research and Therapy, 41*, 1451–1467.

Hurlburt, R. T. (1990). *Sampling normal and schizophrenic inner experience*. New York: Plenum Press.

Hurlburt, R. T. (1993). *Sampling inner experience in disturbed affect*. New York: Plenum Press.

Hurlburt, R. T., & Schwitzgebel, E. (2007). *Describing inner experience? Proponent meets skeptic*. Cambridge, MA: The MIT Press.

Hurley, N. C., Maguire, E. A., & Vargha-Khadem, F. (2011). Patient HC with developmental amnesia can construct future scenarios. *Neuropsychologia, 49*, 3620–3628.

Husserl, E. (1964). *The phenomenology of internal time-consciousness*. Bloomington, IN: Indiana University Press.

Hyman, A. (2007). *The selfseeker*. Exeter, UK: Teignvalley Press.

Irish, M., Addis, D. R., Hodges, J. R., & Piguet, O. (2012). Considering the role of semantic memory in episodic future thinking: Evidence from semantic dementia. *Brain, 135*, 2178–2191.

Ismael, J. T. (2007). *The situated self*. Oxford, UK: Oxford University Press.

Jackson, F. (1986). What Mary didn't know. *Journal of Philosophy, 83*, 291–295.

JAMA Editorial (1950). Lobotomy for relief of pain. *Journal of the American Medical Association, 142*, 35–36.

James, W. (1890). *Principles of psychology (Vol. 1)*. New York: Henry Holt and Company.

James, W. (1909/1996). *A pluralistic universe.* Lincoln, NE: university of Nebraska Press.

Jeans, J. (1943). *The mysterious universe; New revised edition.* New York: The Macmillan Company.

Jeans, J. (1981). *Physics and philosophy.* New York: Dover Publications.

Jensen, M., & Patterson, D. R. (2006). Hypnotic treatment of chronic pain. *Journal of Behavioral Medicine, 29,* 95–124.

Johnstone, H. W. (1970). *The problem of the self.* University Park, PA: The Pennsylvania State University Press.

Kane, R. (2002). *The Oxford handbook of free will.* New York: Oxford University Press.

Kant, I. (1998). *The Cambridge edition of the works of Immanuel Kant; Critique of pure reason.* New York: Cambridge University Press. (Translated by P. Guyer & A. W. Wood).

Keenan, J. M. (1993). An exemplar model can explain Klein and Loftus' results. In T. K. Srull & R. S. Wyer (Eds.), *Advances in social cognition* (Vol. 5; pp. 69–77). Hillsdale, NJ: Erlbaum.

Keenan, J. P. (2003). *The face in the mirror: The search for the origins of consciousness.* New York: HarperCollins Publishers.

Kihlstrom, J. F., Cantor, N., Albright, J. S., Chew, B. R., Klein, S. B., & Niedenthal, P. M. (1988). Information processing and the study of the self. In L. Berkowitz, (Ed.) *Advances in experimental social psychology, Vol. 21: Social psychological studies of the self: Perspectives and programs* (pp. 145–178). Academic Press, Inc, San Diego, CA.

Kihlstrom, J. F., & Klein, S. B. (1994). The self as a knowledge system. In R. S. Wyer & T. K. Srull (Eds.), *Handbook of social cognition. Vol. 1: Basic processes* (pp. 153–208). Hillsdale, NJ: Erlbaum.

Kihlstrom, J. F., & Klein, S. B. (1997). Self-knowledge and self-awareness. In J. G. Snodgrass & R. L. Thompson (Eds.), *The self across psychology: Self-awareness, self-recognition, and the self-concept* (Vol. 818; pp. 5–17). Annals of the New York Academy of Sciences.

Kim, J. (1998). *Philosophy of mind.* Boulder, CO: Westview Press, Inc.

Kim, J. (2000). *Mind in a physical world.* Cambridge, MA: The MIT Press.

Kircher, T., & David, A. (Eds.) (2003). *The self in neuroscience and psychiatry.* New York: Cambridge University Press.

Kirk, R. (1974a). Zombies v. materialists. *Aristotelian Society Proceedings, Supplement, 48,* 135–152.

Kirk, R. (1974b). Sentience and behavior. *Mind, 83,* 43–60.

Kirk, R. (2003). *Mind and body.* Montreal, Canada: McGill-Queen's University Press.

Kitchener, R. F. (Ed.) (1988). *The world of contemporary physics: Does it need a new metaphysics?* Albany, NY: State University of New York Press.

Klein, C. (2011). What pain asymbolia really shows. Published online at philpapers.org/rec/KLEWPA.

Klein, S. B. (2001). A self to remember: A cognitive neuropsychological perspective on how self creates memory and memory creates self. In C. Sedikides & M. B. Brewer (Eds.), *Individual self, relational self, and collective self* (pp. 25–46). Philadelphia, PA: Psychology Press.

Klein, S. B. (2004). The cognitive neuroscience of knowing one's self. In M. A. Gazzaniga (Ed.), *The cognitive neurosciences III* (pp. 1007–1089). Cambridge, MA: MIT Press.

Klein, S. B. (2010). The self: As a construct in psychology and neuropsychological evidence for its multiplicity. *WIREs Cognitive Science, 1,* 172–183.

Klein, S. B. (2012a). The self and its brain. *Social Cognition, 30,* 474–516.

Klein, S. B. (2012b). The self and science: Time for a new approach to the study of human experience. *Current Directions in Psychological Science, 20,* 253–257.

Klein, S. B. (2013a). Making the case that episodic recollection is attributable to operations occurring at retrieval rather than to content stored in a dedicated subsystem of long-term memory. *Frontiers in Behavioral Neuroscience, 7,* 3.*DOI: 103389/fnbeh.2013.00003.*

Klein, S. B. (2013b). The complex act of projecting oneself into the future. *WIREs Cognitive Sciences, 4,* 63–79.

Klein, S.B. (2013b). Social cognition. In B. Kaldis (Ed.), *Encyclopedia of Philosophy and the Social Sciences* (pp. 888-890). Thousand Oaks, CA: Sage Publications.

Klein, S. B. (in press). The sense of diachronic personal identity. *Phenomenology and the Cognitive Sciences.*

Klein, S.B., Altinyazar, V., & Metz, M.A. (2013). *Facets of self in schizophrenia: The reliability and accuracy of trait self-knowledge. Clinical Psychological Science, 1,* 276–289.

Klein, S. B., Babey, S. H., & Sherman, J. W. (1997). The functional independence of trait and behavioral self-knowledge: Methodological considerations and new empirical findings. *Social Cognition, 15,* 183–203.

Klein, S. B., Chan, R. L., & Loftus, J. (1999). Independence of episodic and semantic self-knowledge: The case from autism. *Social Cognition, 17,* 413–436.

Klein, S. B., Cosmides, L., & Costabile, K. (2003). Preserved knowledge of self in a case of Alzheimer's dementia. *Social Cognition, 21,* 157–165.

Klein, S. B., Cosmides, L., Costabile, K. A., & Mei, L. (2002). Is there something special about the self? A neuropsychological case study. *Journal of Research in Personality, 36,* 490–506.

Klein, S. B., Cosmides, L., Murray, E. R., & Tooby, J. (2004). On the acquisition of knowledge about personality traits: Does learning about the self engage different mechanisms than learning about others? *Social Cognition, 22,* 367–390.

Klein, S. B., Cosmides, L., Tooby, J., & Chance, S. (2001). Priming exceptions: A test of the scope hypothesis in naturalistic trait judgments. *Social Cognition, 19,* 443–468.

Klein, S. B., Cosmides, L., Tooby, J., & Chance, S. (2002). Decisions and the evolution of memory: Multiple systems, multiple functions. *Psychological Review, 109,* 306–329.

Klein, S. B., Gabriel, R. H., Gangi, C. E., & Robertson, T. E. (2008). Reflection on the self: A case study of a prosopagnosic patient. *Social Cognition, 26,* 766–777.

Klein, S. B., & Gangi, C. E. (2010). The multiplicity of self: Neuropsychological evidence and its implications for the self as a construct in psychological research. *The Year in Cognitive Neuroscience 2010: Annals of the New York Academy of Sciences, 1191,* 1–15.

Klein, S. B., German, T. P., Cosmides, L., & Gabriel, R. (2004). A theory of autobiographical memory: Necessary components and disorders resulting from their loss. *Social Cognition, 22,* 460–490.

Klein, S. B., & Kihlstrom, J. F. (1986). Elaboration, organization, and the self-reference effect in memory. *Journal of Experimental Psychology: General, 115,* 26–38.

Klein S. B., & Lax, M. L. (2010). The unanticipated resilience of trait self-knowledge in the face of neural damage. *Memory, 18,* 918–948.

Klein, S. B., & Loftus, J. (1990). The role of abstract and exemplar-based knowledge in self-judgments: Implications for a cognitive model of the self. In T. K. Srull and R. S. Wyer (Eds.), *Advances in social cognition* (Vol. 3; pp. 131–139). Hillsdale, NJ: Erlbaum.

Klein, S. B., & Loftus, J. (1993a). The mental representation of trait and autobiographical knowledge about the self. In T. K. Srull & R. S. Wyer (Eds.), *Advances in social cognition* (Vol. 5; pp. 1–49). Hillsdale, NJ: Erlbaum.

Klein., S. B., & Loftus, J. (1993b). *Behavioral experience and trait judgments about the self. Personality & Social Psychology Bulletin, 19,* 740–745.

Klein, S. B., & Loftus, J. (1993c). Some lingering self-doubts: Reply to commentaries. In T. K. Srull and R. S. Wyer (Eds.), *Advances in social cognition* (Vol. 5; pp. 171–180). Hillsdale, NJ: Erlbaum.

Klein, S. B., Loftus, J., & Burton, H. A. (1989). Two self-reference effects: The importance of distinguishing between self-descriptiveness judgments and autobiographical retrieval in self-referent encoding. *Journal of Personality and Social Psychology, 56,* 853–865.

Klein, S. B., Loftus, J., & Kihlstrom, J. F. (1996). Self-knowledge of an amnesic patient: Toward a neuropsychology of personality and social psychology. *Journal of Experimental Psychology: General, 125,* 250–260.

Klein, S. B., Loftus, J., & Kihlstrom, J. F. (2002). Memory and temporal experience: The effects of episodic memory loss on an amnesic patient's ability to remember the past and imagine the future. *Social Cognition, 20,* 353–379.

Klein, S. B., Loftus, J., & Plog, A. E. (1992). Trait judgments about the self: Evidence from the encoding specificity paradigm. *Personality and Social Psychology Bulletin, 18,* 730–735.

Klein, S. B., Loftus, J., Trafton, R. G., & Fuhrman, R. W. (1992). The use of exemplars and abstractions in trait judgments: A model of trait knowledge about the self and others. *Journal of Personality and Social Psychology, 63,* 739–753.

Klein S.B, & Nichols, S. (2012). Memory and the sense of personal identity. *Mind, 121,* 677–702.

Klein, S. B., Robertson, T. E., & Delton, A. W. (2010). Facing the future: Memory as an evolved system for planning future acts. *Memory & Cognition, 38,* 13–22.

Klein, S. B., Roberson, T. E., & Delton, A. W. (2011). The future-orientation of memory: Planning as a key component mediating the high levels of recall found with survival processing. *Memory, 19,* 121–139.

Klein, S. B., Robertson, T. E., Gangi, C. E., & Loftus, J. (2008). The functional independence of trait self-knowledge: Commentary on Sakaki (2007). *Memory, 16,* 556–565.

Klein, S. B., Rozendale, K., & Cosmides, L. (2002). A social-cognitive neuroscience analysis of the self. *Social Cognition, 20,* 105–135.

Klein, S. B., Sherman, R. W., & Loftus, J. (1996). The role of episodic and semantic memory in the development of trait self-knowledge. *Social Cognition, 14,* 277–291.

Koestler, A., & Smythies, J. R. (1967). *Beyond reductionism: The Alpbach Symposium.* Boston, MA: Beacon Press.

Koons, R. C., & Bealer, G. (2010). *The waning of materialism.* New York: Oxford University Press.

Kosso, P. (2007). Scientific understanding. *Foundations of Science, 12,* 173–188.

Krueger, J. W. (2011). The who and how of experience. In M Siderits, E. Thompson, & D. Zahavi (Eds.), *Self, no self: Perspectives from analytical, phenomenological, and Indian traditions* (pp. 27–55). Oxford, UK: Oxford University Press.

Kuhn, T. S. (1962). *The structure of scientific revolutions.* Chicago, IL: The University of Chicago Press.

Kuiper, N. A. (1981). Convergent evidence for the self as a prototype: The "inverted—U RT effect" for self and other judgments. *Personality and Social Psychology Bulletin, 7,* 438–443.

Ladyman, J. (2002). *Understanding philosophy of science.* New York: Routledge.

Lane, T. (2012). Toward an explanatory framework for mental ownership. *Phenomenology and the Cognitive Sciences, 11,* 251–286.

Lange, M. (2002). *An introduction to the philosophy of physics: Locality, fields, energy, and mass.* Malden, MA: Blackwell Publishing.

Leahy, R. L. (1985). *The development of the self.* Orlando, FL: Academic Press, Inc.

Leary, M. R., & Tangney, J. P. (2003). *Handbook of self and identity*. New York: The Guilford Press.

Lecky, P. (1945). *Self-consistency: A theory of personality*. New York: Island Press.

Legrand, D., & Ruby, P. (2009). What is self-specific? Theoretical investigation and critical review of neuroimaging results. *Psychological Review, 116*, 252–282.

Leslie, A. M. (1987). Pretense and representation: The origins of "theory of mind." *Psychological Review, 94*, 412–426.

Libet, B (1993). *Neurophysiology of consciousness: Selected papers and new essays by Benjamin Libet*. Boston, MA: Birkhauser.

Locke, J. (1689-1700/1975). *An essay concerning human understanding*. Oxford, UK: Clarendon Press.

Locksley, A., & Lenauer, M. (1981). Considerations for a theory of self-inference processes. In N. Cantor & J. F. Kihlstrom (Eds.), *Personality, cognition, and social interaction* (pp. 263–277). Hillsdale, NJ: Erlbaum.

Loizou, A. (2000). *Time, embodiment and the self*. Aldershot, UK: Ashgate.

Long, T.A. (1965). *Baier on prefrontal lobotomies and dispositions. Southern Journal of Philosophy, 3*, 131–137.

Lord, C. G. (1993). The "social self" component of trait knowledge about the self. In T. K. Srull & R. S Wyer (Eds.), *Advances in social cognition* (Vol. 5; pp. 91–100). Hillsdale, NJ: Erlbaum.

Lovejoy, A. O. (1930). *The revolt against dualism*. New York: W. W. Norton & Company, Inc.

Lowe, E. J. (1996). *Subjects of experience*. Cambridge, UK: Cambridge University Press.

Lowe, E. J. (2008). A defense of non-Cartesian substance dualism. In A. Antonietti, A. Corradini, and E. J. Lowe (Eds.), *Psycho-physical dualism: An interdisciplinary approach* (pp. 167–184). Boulder, CO: Rowman & Littlefield Publishers, Inc.

Loy, D. L. (1988). *Nonduality: A study in comparative philosophy*. Amherst, NY: Humanity Books.

Lund, D. H. (2005). *The conscious self*. Amherst, NY: Humanity Books.

Madell, G. (1984). *The identity of the self*. Edinburgh, UK: Edinburgh University Press.

Margenau, H. (1950). *The nature of physical reality*. New York: McGraw Hill.

Marganau, H. (1984). *The miracle of existence*. Woodbridge, CT: Ox Bow Press.

Markus, H. (1977). Self-schemata and processing information about the self. *Journal of Personality and Social Psychology, 35*, 63–78.

Martin, C. B. (2008). *The mind in nature*. Oxford, UK: Oxford University Press.

Martin, E. (1971). Verbal learning theory and independent retrieval phenomena. *Psychological Review, 78*, 314–332.

Martinelli, P. Sperduti. M. & Piolino, P. (2013). Neural substrates of the self-memory system: New insights from a meta-analysis. *Human Brain Mapping, 34*, 1515–1529.

Martinelli, P., Anssens, A., Sperduti, & Piolino, P. (in press). The influence of normal aging and Alzheimer's disease in autobiographical memory highly related to the self. *Neuropsychology.*

McGinn, C. (1991). *The problem of consciousness: Essays toward a resolution.* Oxford, UK: Blackwell Publishers.

McAdams, D. P. (1993). *The stories we live by: Personal myths and the making of the self.* New York: William Morrow.

McGlynn, S. M., & Kaszniak, A. W. (1991). Unawareness of deficits in dementia and schizophrenia. In G. P. Prigatano & D. L. Schacter (Eds.), *Awareness of deficit after brain injury: Clinical and theoretical perspectives* (pp. 84–110). New York: Oxford University Press.

McGlynn, S. M., & Schacter, D. L. (1989). Unawareness of deficits in neuropsychological syndromes. *Journal of Clinical & Experimental Neuropsychology, 11,* 143–205.

Medford, N., Sierra, M. Baker, D., & David, A. S. (2005). Understanding and treating depersonalisation disorder. *Advances in Psychiatric Treatment, 11,* 92–100.

Meixner, U. (2005). Physicalism, dualism and intellectual honesty. *Dualism Review, 1,* 1–20.

Meixner, U. (2008). The reductio of reductive and non-reductive materialism—and a new start. In A. Antonietti, A. Corradini, & E. J. Lowe (Eds.), *Psycho-physical dualism: An interdisciplinary approach* (pp. 143–166). Boulder, CO: Rowman & Littlefield Publishers, Inc.

Melnick, A. (2009). *Kant's theory of the self.* New York: Routledge.

Melnyk, A. (2003). *A physicalist manifesto: Thoroughly modern materialism.* Cambridge, MA: Cambridge University Press.

Melzack, P., & Wall, R. (1985). *The challenge of pain; Revised edition.* New York, NY: Basic Books.

Metzinger, T. (2009). *The ego tunnel: The science of mind and the myth of the self.* New York: Basic Books.

Mills, M. A. (1997). Narrative identity and dementia: A study of emotion and narrative in older people with dementia. *Ageing & Society, 17,* 673–698.

Mills, M. A. (1998). *Narrative identity and dementia.* Aldershot, UK: Ashgate Publications, Ltd.

Mischel, T. (1977). *The self: Psychological and philosophical issues.* Oxford, UK: Basil Blackwell.

Mitchell, J. (1999). *Measurement in psychology: A critical history of a methodological concept.* Cambridge, UK: Cambridge University Press.

Mograbi, D. C., Brown, R. G., & Morris, R. G. (2009). Anosognosia in Alzheimer's disease—The petrified self. *Consciousness and Cognition, 18,* 989–1003.

Morris, R. G., & Mograbi, D. C. (2013). Anosognosia, autobiographical memory and self knowledge in Alzheimer's disease. *Cortex*

Nagel, E., & Newman, J. R. (2001). *Gödel's proof, revised edition*. New York: New York University Press.

Nagel, T. (1974). What is it like to be a bat? *Philosophical Review, 83*, 435–450.

Nagel, T. (2012). *Mind and cosmos: Why the materialist neo-Darwinian conception of nature is almost certainly wrong*. Oxford, UK: Oxford University Press.

Neely, J. H. (1989). Experimental dissociations and the episodic/semantic memory distinction. In H. L. Roediger & F. I. M. Craik (Eds.), *Varieties of memory and consciousness: Essays in honor of Endel Tulving* (pp. 229–270). Hillsdale, NJ: Lawrence Erlbaum Associates.

Neisser, U. (1988). Five kinds of self–knowledge. *Philosophical Psychology, 1*, 35–39.

Neisser, U., & Fivush, R. (1994). *The remembering self: Construction and accuracy in the self-narrative*. Cambridge, UK: Cambridge University Press.

Nelson, K. (1989). *Narratives from the crib*. Cambridge, MA: Harvard university Press.

Nelson, K. (2003). Narrative and self, myth and memory: Emergence of the cultural self. In R. Fivush & C. A. Haden (Eds.), *Autobiographical memory and the construction of a narrative self: Developmental and cultural perspectives* (pp. 3–28. Mahwah, NJ: Lawrence Erlbaum Publishers.

Neuhouser, F. (1990). *Fichte's theory of subjectivity*. New York: Cambridge University Press.

Northoff, G. (2004). *Philosophy of the brain*. Philadelphia, PA: John Benjamins Publishing Company.

Olson, E. T. (1997). *The human animal: Personal identity without psychology*. New York: Oxford University Press.

Olson, E. T. (1999). There is no problem of the self. In S. Gallagher & J. Shear (Eds.), *Models of the self* (pp. 49–61). Thorverton, UK: Imprint Academic.

Olson, E. T. (2007). *What are we? A study in personal ontology*. Oxford, UK: Oxford University Press.

Owen, A. M., Coleman, M. R., Boly, M., Davis, M. H., Laureys, S., & Pickard, J. D. (2006). Detecting awareness in the vegetative state. *Science, 313*, 1402.

Papa-Grimaldi, A. (1998). *Time and reality*. Aldershot, UK: Ashgate.

Parkin, A. J. (1993). *Memory: Phenomena, experiment and theory*. Cambridge, MA: Blackwell.

Penrose, R. (1989). *The emperor's new mind: Concerning computers, minds and the laws of physics*. Oxford, UK: Oxford University Press.

Penrose, R. (2005). *The road to reality: A complete guide to the laws of the universe*. New York: Alfred A. Knopf.

Perner, J.,& Ruffman, T. (1994). *Episodic memory and autonoetic consciousness: Developmental evidence and a theory of childhood amnesia. Journal of Experimental Child Psychology, 59*, 516–548.

Perry, J. (1975). *Personal identity*. Los Angeles, CA: University of California Press.

Persson, I (2005). Self-doubt: Why we are not identical to things of any kind. In G. Strawson (Ed.), *The self?* (pp. 26–44). Malden, MA: Blackwell Publishing.

Pesic, P. (2002). *Seeing double: Shared identities in physics, philosophy, and literature.* Cambridge, MA: The MIT Press.

Pessoa, L., Thompson. E., & Noë, A. (1998). Filling-in is for finding out. *Behavioral and Brain Sciences, 21*, 781–796.

Phillips, M. L., Medford, N., Senior, C., Bullmore, E. T., Suckling, J., Brammer, M. J., Andrew, C., Sierra, M., Williams, S. C. R., & David, A. S. (2001). Depersonalization disorder: Thinking without feeling. *Psychiatry Research: Neuroimaging Section, 108*, 145–160.

Picard, L., Mayor-Dubois, C., Maeder, P., Kalenzaga, S., Abram, M., Duval, C., Eustache, F., Roulet-Perez, E., & Piolino, P. (2013). Functional independence within the self-memory system: Insight from two cases of developmental amnesia. *Cortex, 49*, 1463–1481

Place, U. T. (1956). Is consciousness a brain process? *British Journal of Psychology, 47*, 44–50.

Planck, M. (1925/1993). *A survey of physical theory.* New York: Dover Publications.

Poincaré, H. (1952. *Science and hypothesis.* New York: Dover Publications, Inc.

Popper, K. R. (1994). *Knowledge and the body-mind problem: In defense of interaction.* London: Routledge.

Prebble, S., Addis, D. R., Tippett, L. J. (in press). Autobiographical memory and sense of self. *Psychological Bulletin.*

Prigatano, G. P., & Schacter, D. L. (Eds.) (1991). *Awareness of deficit after brain injury.* Oxford, UK: Oxford University Press.

Proust, M. (1981). *Remembrance of things past, Volume 1.* New York, NY: Random House. (Translation by C.K. Scott Moncrieff and T. Kilmartin).

Race, E., Keane, M. N., & Verfaellie, M. (2011). Medial temporal lobe damage causes deficits in episodic memory and episodic future thinking not attributable to deficits in narrative construction. *Journal of Neuroscience, 31*, 10262–10269.

Rankin, K. P., Baldwin, E., Pace-Savitsky, C., Kramer, J. H., & Miller, B. L. (2005). Self awareness and personality change in dementia. *Journal of Neurology, Neurosurgery, and Psychiatry, 76*, 632–639.

Rathbone, C. J., Moulin, C. J. A., & Conway, M. A. (2009). Autobiographical memory and amnesia: Using conceptual knowledge to ground the self. *Neurocase, 15*, 405–418.

Redman, S. J. (1990). Quantal analysis of synaptic potentials in neurons of the central nervous system. *Physiological Review, 70*, 165–198.

Reichenbach, H. (1942/1970). *From Copernicus to Einstein.* New York: Dover Publications, Inc.

Reichenbach, H. (1951). *The rise of scientific philosophy.* Berkeley, CA: University of California Press.

REFERENCES

Renoult, L., Davidson, P. S. R., Palombo, D. J., Moscovitch. M., & Levine, B. (2012). Personal semantics: At the crossroads of semantic and episodic memory. *Trends in Cognitive Sciences, 16,* 550–558.

Rescher, N. (1984). *The limits of science.* Berkeley, CA: University of California Press.

Rescher, N. (1996). *Process metaphysics.* Albany, NY: State university of New York Press.

Rescher, N. (1997). *Objectivity: The obligations of impersonal reason.* Notre Dame, IN: University of Notre Dame Press.

Rescher, N. (2000). *Process philosophy: A survey of basic issues.* Pittsburgh, PA: University of Pittsburgh Press.

Reutens, S., Nielson, O., & Sachdev, P. (2010). Depersonalisation disorder. *Current Opinion in Psychiatry, 23,* 278–283.

Ricard, M., & Thuan, T. X. (2001). *The quantum and the lotus.* New York: Three Rivers Press.

Robinson, M. F., & Freeman, W. (1954). *Psychosurgery and the self.* New York: Grune & Stratton.

Roediger, H. L., & Blaxton, T. A. (1987). Effects of varying modality, surface features, and retention interval on priming in word-fragment completion. *Memory & Cognition, 15,* 379–388.

Roediger, H. L., Weldon, M. S., & Challis, B. H. (1989). Explaining dissociations between implicit and explicit measures of retention: A processing account. In H. L. Roediger & F. I. M. Craik (Eds.), *Varieties of memory and consciousness: Essays in honor of Endel Tulving* (pp. 3–41). Hillsdale, NJ: Erlbaum.

Rosenberg, M. (1979/1986). *Conceiving the self.* Malabar, FL: Robert E. Krieger Publishing Company.

Rosenthal, D. M. (1991). *The nature of mind.* Oxford, UK: Oxford University Press.

Rossman, N. (1991). *Consciousness: Separation and integration.* Albany, NY: State University of New York Press.

Rosser, J. B. (1936). Extensions of some theorems of Gödel and Church. *Journal of Symbolic Logic, 1,* 87–91.

Rubin, D. C. (1986). *Autobiographical memory.* New York: Cambridge University Press.

Russell, B. (1912/1999). *The problems of philosophy.* Mineola, NY: Dover Publications.

Russell, B. (1913/1992). *Theory of knowledge.* New York: Routledge.

Ryle, G. (1949). *The concept of mind.* New York: Barnes & Noble.

Samsonovich, A. V., & Nadel, L. (2005). Fundamental principles and mechanisms of the conscious self. *Cortex, 41,* 669–689.

Schacter, D. L., & Tulving, E. (Eds.) (1994). *Memory systems 1994.* Cambridge, MA: MIT Press.

Schell, T. L., Klein, S. B., & Babey, S. H. (1996). Testing a hierarchical model of self-knowledge. *Psychological Science, 7,* 170–173.

Schechtman, M. (1996). *The constitution of selves*. Ithaca, NY: Cornell University Press.

Schwerin, A. (2012). *Hume's labyrinth: A search for the self*. Newcastle upon Tyne, UK: Cambridge Scholar's Publishing.

Sedikides, C., & Brewer, M. B. (2001). *Individual self, relational self, collective self*. Philadelphia, PA: Psychology Press.

Sedikides, C., & Spencer, S. J. (2007). *The self*. New York: Psychology Press.

Seigler, I. C., Dawson, D. V., & Welsh, K. A., (1994). Caregiver ratings of personality change in Alzheimer's Disease patients: A replication. *Psychology and Aging, 9*, 464–466.

Sellers, W. (1963). *Science, perception and reality*. London: Routledge & Kegan Paul Ltd.

Shallis, M. (1983). *On time: An investigation into scientific knowledge and human experience*. New York: Schocken Books.

Sherman, J. W. (1996). Development and mental representation of stereotypes. *Journal of Personality and Social Psychology, 70*, 1126–1141.

Sherman, J. W., & Klein, S. B. (1994). Development and representation of personality impressions. *Journal of Personality and Social Psychology, 67*, 972–983.

Sherman, J. W., Klein, S. B., Laskey, A., & Wyer, N. A. (1998). Intergroup bias in group judgment processes: The role of behavioral memories. *Journal of Experimental Social Psychology, 34*, 51–65.

Shewmon, D. A., Holmes, G. L., & Byrne, P. A. (1999). Consciousness in congenitally decorticate children: Developmental vegetative state as self-fulfilling prophecy. *Developmental Medicine & Child Neurology, 41*, 364–374.

Shoemaker, S. (1970). Persons and their past. *American Philosophical Quarterly, 7*, 269–285.

Shommers, W. (1994). *Space and time, matter and mind*. River Edge, NJ: World Scientific Publishing Company.

Siderits, M. (2003). *Personal identity and Buddhist philosophy*. Hampshire, UK: Ashgate Publishing Limited.

Siderits, M. (2011). Buddhas as zombies: A Buddhist reduction of subjectivity. In M. Siderits, E. Thompson, & D. Zahavi (Eds.) (2011). *Self, no self: Perspectives from analytical, phenomenological and Indian traditions* (pp. 308–331). Oxford, UK: Oxford University Press.

Siderits, M., Thompson, E., & Zahavi, D. (2011). *Self, no self: Perspectives from analytical phenomenological and Indian traditions*. Oxford, UK: Oxford University Press.

Sierra, M., Baker, D., Medford, N., & David, A. S. (2005). Unpacking the depersonalization syndrome: An exploratory factor analysis on the Cambridge Depersonalization Scale. *Psychological Medicine, 35*, 1523–1532.

Sierra, M., & Berrios, G. E. (1997). Depersonalization: A conceptual history. *History of Psychiatry, 8*, 213–229.

Silva, J. A., & Leong, G. B. (1992). The Capgras syndrome in paranoid schizophrenics. *Psychopathology, 25*, 147–153.

Simeon, D. (2004). Depersonalisation disorder: A contemporary overview. *CNS Drugs, 18*, 343–354.

Simeon, D., & Abugel, J. (2006). *Feeling unreal: Depersonalisation disorder and the loss of the self.* Oxford, UK: Oxford University Press.

Singer, J. A., & Salovey, P. (1993). *The remembered self: Emotion and memory in personality.* New York: the Free Press.

Sinkman, A. (2008). The syndrome of Capgras. *Psychiatry: Interpersonal and Biological Processes, 71*, 371–378.

Slors, M. (2001). *The diachronic mind: An essay on personal identity, psychological continuity and the mind-body problem.* Boston, MA: Kluwer Academic Publishers.

Smith, E. R., & Zarate, M. A. (1992). Exemplar-based models of social judgment. *Psychological Review, 99*, 3–21.

Smith, Q. (2003). Why cognitive scientists cannot ignore quantum mechanics. In Q. Smith & A. Jokic (Eds.), *Consciousness: New philosophical perspectives* (pp. 409–446). Oxford, UK: Oxford University Press.

Snodgrass, J. G., & Thompson, R. L. (1997). *The self across psychology: Self-awareness, self-recognition, and the self-concept. Annals of the New York Academy of Sciences, 818*, New York, NY; The New York Academy of Sciences.

Sorabji, R. (2006). *Self: Ancient and modern insights about individuality, life, and death.* Chicago, USA: The University of Chicago Press.

Spencer Brown, G. (1957). *Probability and scientific inference.* London: Longmans, Green and Co.

Sperber, D., & Wilson, D. (1995). *Relevance: Communication and cognition (2nd ed.).* Oxford, UK: Blackwell.

Stanford, P. K. (2006). *Exceeding our grasp: Science, history and the problem of unconceived alternatives.* New York: Oxford University Press.

Stapp, H. P. (1993). *Mind, matter, and quantum mechanics.* New York: Springer-Verlag.

Stapp, H. P. (2011). *Mindful universe (2nd ed.).* New York: Springer-Verlag.

Stephens, G. L., & Graham, G. (2000). *When self-consciousness breaks: Alien voices and inserted thoughts.* Cambridge, MA: The MIT Press.

Stern, D. (1985). *The interpersonal world of the infant.* New York: Basic Books.

Stove, D. (2001). *Scientific irrationalism: Origins of a postmodern cult.* London: Translation Publishers.

Strauss, J., & Goethals, G. R. (1991). *The self: Interdisciplinary approaches.* New York: Springer Verlag.

Strawson, G. (2005). *The self?* Oxford, UK: Blackwell Publishing.

Strawson, G. (2009). *Selves: An essay in revisionary metaphysics.* New York: Oxford University Press.

Strawson, G. (2011a). *The evident connection.* Oxford, UK: Oxford University Press.

Strawson, G. (2011b). *Locke on personal identity: Consciousness and concernment.* Princeton, NJ: Princeton University Press.

Stroud, B. (2000). *The quest for reality: Subjectivism and the metaphysics of color.* New York: Oxford University Press.

Stuss, D. T. (1991). Self, awareness and the frontal lobes: A neuropsychological perspective. In J. Strauss & G. R. Goethals (Eds.), *The self: Interdisciplinary approaches* (pp. 255–278). New York: Springer-Verlag.

Suddendorf, T., & Corballis, M. C. (1997). Mental time travel and the evolution of the human mind. *Genetic, Social, and General Psychology Monographs, 123*(2), 133–167.

Swinburne, R. (1997). *The evolution of the soul.* Oxford, UK: Clarendon Press.

Swinburne, R. (2011). *Free will and modern science.* New York: Oxford University Press.

Swinburne, R. (2013). *Mind, brain, and free will.* Oxford, UK: Oxford University Press.

Symonds, P. M. (1951). *The ego and the self.* New York: Appleton-Century-Crofts, Inc.

Symons, C. S., & Johnson, B. T. (1997). The self-reference effect in memory: A meta-analysis. *Psychological Bulletin, 121,* 371–394.

Synofzik, M., Vosgerau, G., & Newen, A. (2008). I move, therefore I am: A new theoretical framework to investigate agency and ownership. *Consciousness and Cognition, 17,* 411–424.

Tallis, R. (2008). *The enduring significance of Parmenides: Unthinkable thought.* London: Continuum International Publishing Group.

Terrace, H. S., & Metcalfe, J. (Eds.) (2005). *The missing link in cognition: Origins of self-reflective consciousness.* New York: Oxford University Press.

Teuber, H. L. (1955). Physiological psychology. *Annual Review of Psychology, 6,* 267–296.

Thompson, I. J. (2008). Discreet degrees within and between nature and mind. In A. Antonietti, A. Corradini, & E. J. Lowe (Eds.), *Psycho-physical dualism: An interdisciplinary approach* (pp. 99–123). Boulder, CO: Rowman & Littlefield Publishers.

Toyabe, S., Takahiro, S., Ueda, M., Muneyuki, E., & Sano, M. (2010). Information heat engine: converting information to energy by feedback control. *Nature Physics, 6,* 988–992.

Trusted, J. (1991). *Physics and metaphysics: Theories of space and time.* New York: Routledge.

Trusted, J. (1999). *The mystery of matter.* New York: St. Martin's Press.

Tulving, E. (1983). *Elements of episodic memory.* New York: Oxford University Press.

Tulving, E. (1985). Memory and consciousness. *Canadian Psychology/Psychologie Canadienne, 26,* 1–12.

Tulving, E. (1993). Self-knowledge of an amnesic individual is represented abstractly. In T. K. Srull & R. S. Wyer (Eds.), *Advances in social cognition* (Vol. 5; pp. 147–156). Hillsdale, NJ: Erlbaum.

Tulving, E. (1995). Organization of memory: *Quo vadis?* In M. S. Gazzaniga (Ed.). *The cognitive neurosciences* (pp. 839–847). Cambridge, MA: MIT Press.

Tulving, E., & Schacter, D. L. (1990). *Priming and human memory systems. Science, 247,* 301–306.

Tulving, E., & Szpunar, K. K. (2012). Does the future exist? In B. Levine and F. L. M. Craik (Eds.), *Mind and the frontal lobes* (pp. 248–263). New York: Oxford University Press.

Uttal, W. R. (202008). *Time, space, and number in physics and psychology.* Cornwall-on-Hudson, NY: Sloan Publishing.

Valera, F. J., Thompson, E., & Rosch, E. (1993). *The embodied mind: Cognitive science and human experience.* Cambridge, MA: The MIT Press.

Vallar, G., & Ronchi, R. (2009). Somatoparaphrenia: A body delusion. A review of the neuropsychological literature. *Experimental Brain Research, 192,* 533–551.

van Fraasen, B. C. (2005). Transcendence of the ego (The non-existent knight). In G. Strawson (Ed.), *The self?* (pp. 87–110). Malden, MA: Blackwell Publishing.

van Inwagen, P. (2002). *Metaphysics (2nd ed.).* Cambridge, MA: Westview Press.

Vargha-Khadem, F., Gadian, D. G., Watkins, K. E., Connelly, A., Van Paesschen, W., & Mishkin, M. (1997). Differential effects of early hippocampal pathology on episodic and semantic memory. *Science, 277,* 376–380.

Vauhinger, H. (1925). *The philosophy of "as if".* New York: Harcourt, Brace, & Company, Inc.

Vierkant, T. (2003). *Is the self real?* London: Transaction Publishers.

Von Baeyer, H. C. (2003). *Information: The new language of science.* Cambridge, MA: Harvard University Press.

Wallace, R. A. (2003). *Choosing reality: A Buddhist view of physics and the mind.* Ithaca, N. Y.: Snow Lion Publications.

Wang, H. (1996). *A logical journey: From Gödel to philosophy.* Cambridge, MA: The MIT Press.

Wheeler, M. A., Stuss, D. T., & Tulving, E. (1997). Toward a theory of episodic memory: The frontal lobes and autonoetic consciousness. *Psychological Bulletin, 121,* 331–354.

White, S. L. (1991). *The unity of the self.* Cambridge, MA: MIT Press.

Wilson, B. A., & Wearing, D. (1995). Trapped in time: Profound autobiographical memory loss following thalamic stroke. In R. Campbell & M. A. Conway (Eds.), *Broken memories: Case studies in memory impairment* (pp. 31–44). Cambridge, USA: Blackwell.

Wisdom, J. (1968). *Other minds.* Berkeley, CA: University of California Press.

Wright, C., Smith, B. C., & Macdonald, C. (1998). *Knowing our own minds.* Oxford, UK: Oxford University Press.

Yao, Z. (2005). *The Buddhist theory of self-cognition.* New York: Routledge.

Young, K., & Saver, J. L. (2001). The neurology of narrative. *Substance, 30,* 72–84.

Zahavi, D. (1999). *Self-awareness and alterity: A phenomenological investigation.* Evanston, IL: Northwestern University Press.

Zahavi, D. (2005). *Subjectivity of selfhood: Investigating the first-person perspective.* Cambridge, MA: The MIT Press.

Zahavi, D. (2011). The experiential self: Objections and clarifications. In M Siderits, E. Thompson, & D. Zahavi (Eds.), *Self, no self: Perspectives from analytical phenomenological and Indian traditions* (pp. 56–78). Oxford, UK: Oxford University Press.

Zahn, R., Talazko, J., & Ebert, D. (2008). Loss of sense of self-ownership for perceptions of objects in a case of right inferior temporal, parieto-occipital and precentral hypometabolism. *Psychopathology, 41*, 397–402.

INDEX

Albahari, M., 100
Alzheimer's dementia studies, 35–38, 44
Amnesia studies, 31–35, 44, 86–88, 124n1
Anosodiaphoria, 96
Anosognosia, 96–99
Anoxia studies, 33–35, 86–88, 124n1
Antonietti, A., 70
Autism studies, 38–44
Autobiographical memory cueing task,
    31–32, 39
Awareness, 76–77

Babinski, J., 96
Bisiach, E., 97
Bohr, Niels, 58
Brain trauma studies, 32–38, 44, 98,
    103–9, 125nn5–7
Brentano, F., 123n1
Brown, N. R., 27
Bundle theory of perception, 121n2, 121n5
Byrne, P. A., 83

Capgras syndrome, 125n4
Cartesian substance dualism, 73
Causal closure under the phsycial, 63–64
Causation, 58–64, 124n4
Chalmers, D. J., xvi, 79, 113
Chan, R. L., 39
Chisholm, Roderick, 47
Consciousness, 9–10, 79–80

Copenhagen Complementarity, 65
Cosmides, L., 40, 41
Costabile, K. A., 40
Crovitz, H. F., 31

Danziger, K., 64
Decorticate patient studies, 83–84
Definition-generation control task, 27–28
Depersonalization, 92, 95, 99–100, 125n4
Derealization, 125n4
Descartes, Rene, 48
Descartes' Dilemma, 63
Determinism, xi–xiii
Developmental dissociations (autism)
    studies, 38–44
Dewey, J., 67
Dissociation
    developmental dissociations (autism)
        studies, 38–44
    in memory ownership loss, 103–9,
        125nn5–9
    in perceptual ownership loss, 101–3
Dissociations
    single, 85–88, 124n1
Dualism
    Cartesian substance, 73
    concepts of self, 4–5, 113, 121nn4–5
    nature of reality, 72–75, 124n7
    wave/particle duality principle, 56, 65
Dunn, J. C., 29

INDEX

Hume, D., 121n2, 121n5, 123n1
Hurlburt, R. T., 82

Immateriality
  terminology, usage, 16–17
Incompleteness theorem, xi–xii, xiv,
  120n1
Inductive pessimism, 124n5
Inference
  in memory ownership loss, 103–9,
    125nn5–9
  in perceptual ownership loss, 101–3
  role of generally, 109–10
Information exchange, 60–62
Introspective reports, 82–83, 114–15

James, William, 9, 13, 15, 20, 49, 73, 79, 81,
  104, 112, 121n4

Kant, Immanuel, 2, 123n2
Keenan, J. M., 27
Kihlstrom, J. F., 31
Kirk, R., 79
Kirsner, K., 29
Klein, C., 94, 95
Klein, S. B., 4, 21–31, 33–35, 39–42, 83,
  85–90, 103–109, 124n1

Laplace, Pierre-Simon, xi
Light cone concept, 54–55
Locke, John, 12, 79
Loftus, J., 29, 30, 31, 39
Long term memory. *see also* memory
  declarative, 18
  episodic *vs.* semantic, 18–19, 122n6
  procedural, 17–18

Martin, C. B., 117
Materialism, xiv–xv, 7, 13, 51–52, 60, 116,
  126n1
Mei, L., 40
Meixner, U., xiv, 2, 52, 63, 116, 126n1
Memory
  autobiographical memory cueing task,
    31–32, 39
  dissociation in memory ownership loss,
    103–9, 125nn5–9

inference in memory ownership loss,
  103–9, 125nn5–9
long-term (*see* long term memory)
ownership loss studies, 103–9,
  125nn5–9
quasi-memory, 103–9, 125nn5–9
reduction of, 68, 69
Mind/body identity doctrine, 54–55
Murray, E. R., 41

Nagarjuna, 65
Nagel, T., 75, 119
Neuro-cognitive aspects of self, 6, 20–23,
  43–45, 78–79, 122n1, 124n1

Ontological self
  awareness, 76–77
  Cartesian substance dualism, 73
  causal closure under the physical,
    63–64
  causation, 58–64, 124n4
  decorticate patient studies, 83–84
  defined, 4–7, 46–49, 121nn4–5,
    123nn1–3
  dualistic nature of reality, 72–75,
    124n7
  energy conservation, exchange, 58–64,
    124n4
  functional independence (*see* functional
    independence)
  inference of, 47–48
  information exchange, 60–62
  light cone concept, 54–55
  memory, reduction of, 68, 69
  as metaphysical (non-material),
    49–52
  mind/body identity doctrine, 54–55
  objectification, quantification, 66–69,
    84–85, 113–14
  objectivity in study of, 46–47
  pain experience, 68–70
  personal ownership (*see* personal
    ownership)
  phenomenology, 69–72
  Planck length, 55
  properties of, 48–49, 76–78, 111–12,
    123nn2–3

151

as subjective entity, 2–3
two aspects theory, 4–5, 76–80, 113,
    121nn4
Self-awareness. *see* ontological self
Self-recognition, 111
Sense, experience, 13–14
Shewmon, D. A., 83
Single dissociations, 85–88, 124n1
Stimulus-response connection, ix–xi
Strawson, G., 121n3
String theory, 124n6
Stroud, B., 66
Subatomic particles, 56, 57, 65, 124n6
Subjectivity (personal experience), 65–68,
    71, 124n6. *see also* ontological self
Swinburne, R., 57
Szpunar, K. K., 72–74

Terminology, 8–17
Thought insertion, 95–96
Thuan, T. X., 114
Tooby, J., 41
Trait self-knowledge studies, 29–45
Transcendental Deduction (Kant), 123n2
Transfer-appropriate processing, 29
Trusted, J., 58
Tulving, E., 12, 18, 72–74

Valera, F. J., 71

Wave/particle duality principle,
    56, 65

Zahavi, D., 69, 71
Zahn, R., 101–2